Basic Skills in English

McDougal, Littell & Company

Evanston. Illinois

This Teacher's Manual was prepared with the assistance of

Janet Gibson

Nancy Kellman

Marilyn M. Sherman

Editorial Director: Joy Littell
Managing Editor: Kathleen Laya
Associate Editor: Mary Schafer

ISBN: 0-88343-784-8

CONTENTS

Special Features of
Basic Skills in English

Scope and Purpose of the Series

Basic Skills in English is an English series for grades 7-12 designed to help students master essential writing and other language skills. The series is suitable for students of all ability levels, but is particularly appropriate for students reading below grade level. While each successive book in the series takes into account the increasing maturity of the student, the reading level remains within the fifth- to sixth-grade range. This text (Book 4) is recommended for use at grade 10.

Organization of Each Book

Each book in the series is divided into two main parts:

1. **Composition.** The first half of the book includes sections on vocabulary development, sentence improvement, and the writing of paragraphs, compositions, and letters. It also includes sections on those skills that support the student in writing and editing his or her own work: dictionary use, library use, and the use of important reference works.

2. **Handbook.** The second half of the book includes sections on grammar and usage, capitalization, punctuation, and spelling.

Key Features of the COMPOSITION Part

1. **The lessons follow a simple, consistent plan.** Each lesson deals with a single topic or skill and is short enough (usually two pages) to insure completion of the instruction in one class period. The students follow this plan for each lesson:

> **Here's the Idea** This presents to the students the idea or skill to be learned in the lesson.
> **Check It Out** The students react to the idea, and test it to be sure that they understand it.
> **Try Your Skill** The students apply the idea or skill in a short structured exercise.
> **Keep This in Mind** A boxed summary reinforces the students' understanding of the main idea of the lesson.
> **Now Write** The students perform an independent writing assignment for which they are now well prepared.

2. **The lessons emphasize the steps in the process of writing.** Writing is a mystery for many students; they do not understand what is expected of them. In these lessons the students can actually see the development of a piece of writing. The lessons move from selecting a topic, listing specific details, organizing notes, writing a draft, revising and editing, to making a final copy. This step-by-step process unravels the mysteries of writing and helps students to achieve a satisfying measure of success in composition.

3. **The lessons are progressive.** Within each book the instruction moves from work with smaller units of writing to larger units. It moves from choosing the right word (vocabulary development) to writing sentences, to writing paragraphs, to writing a composition or a report. Within each section, it follows closely the steps in the process of writing, recognizing the students' need to know how to begin a piece of writing, how to develop it, and how to complete it. Within each lesson, it moves from an explanation of an idea to its application.

4. **The lessons are practical.** The skills and techniques presented are useful to the student now and in later life. They have been selected specifically for their utility. The examples that illustrate them and the assignments that provide practice on them have been chosen to demonstrate how they can help the student in both academic and work settings.

5. **The lessons are illustrated with many examples.** These include not only examples of finished work but also examples of work at various stages in the process of writing, so that the students can see at first hand what is expected as an end result. The examples present work that the students can expect to equal, not work that is so far beyond their abilities that it intimidates more than it inspires.

6. **The lessons are organized to insure success.** The students are never asked to do something that has not been taught. Furthermore, exercises based on a concept or skill do not require that the students have fully mastered the concept or skill. The tone of the instruction throughout is one of encouragement, reflecting confidence in the students' abilities.

Use of Writing Folders

Throughout this series, students are asked to keep their independent **Now Write** assignments in folders. Depending on your school's policy, you may issue these folders to students or ask them to purchase their own. Both you and your students need to keep track of writing assignments in separate writing folders for reasons that are as practical as they are educationally sound:

1. Students should be encouraged to write in the classroom and to keep assignments there.
2. Both you and your students need a permanent record of assignments completed. Assignments can be compared in order to see measurable progress, and in order to determine grades.
3. As students see a growing body of material that reflects their own ideas and interests, writing folders become special, personal collections. In this way, writing becomes a more positive experience.
4. Labeled with the title of each lesson, each writing assignment is keyed to the text. At any time, you or your students may refer to a lesson for review of the specific skill or concept taught.

Key Features of the HANDBOOK Part

1. **The Handbook part of *Basic Skills in English* presents a clear, comprehensive treatment of grammar, usage, capitalization, punctuation, and spelling.** The text is organized for direct teaching; it is also organized in such a way that students can easily use the Handbook independently for reference.

2. **Each Section is a self-contained unit.** Each section is devoted to a single topic, and all information on that topic is presented together in the Section. Everything about nouns is presented in one Section, everything about pronouns in another Section, and so on.

3. **Each Section has a wealth of exercises.** Every section is divided into Parts, each Part dealing with a separate skill. Each Part concludes with exercises on the skill developed. Wherever possible, there are several exercises using a variety of approaches to the same skill. Each Section is followed by a cumulative review of all the skills developed in that Section. This quantity and variety of exercises provides the teacher with ample material for practice, reinforcement, and review.

4. **The typographic arrangement is clear and attractive.** Type and open space have been used to set off definitions and examples so as to make them easy to find and easy to read.

This Teacher's Manual

There are three sections in the Teacher's Manual:

1. **This Introduction,** entitled "Special Features of *Basic Skills in English*."

2. **Teaching Suggestions for Composition (pages 2-83) and Teaching Suggestions for the Handbook (pages 85-173).** The Teaching Suggestions include these elements:

Section Objectives This is a list of the skills that each student is expected to master in the study of the Section.

Preparing the Students This is a lesson designed to orient the students to the subject of the Section.

Presenting the Lesson These are step-by-step suggestions for teaching each Part in the Section, stressing points of emphasis and offering suggestions for use of the exercises.

Optional Practice This is an additional teaching resource for drill or review of materials.

Extending the Lesson This is an enrichment lesson or exercise relating the material discussed in the Part to a new topic, or approaching the material in a new way.

3. **Keys to Exercises.** These begin on page 175.

Related Materials

Besides the exercises provided in the student text and the Teacher's Manual, additional supporting materials are available. These are coodinated with the Sections in *Basic Skills in English, Book 4*.

Practice Book   This consumable workbook provides additional practice and reinforcement keyed to the Sections in the text.

Diagnostic and Mastery Tests   This consumable booklet includes pretests for Sections for which students may be expected to have prior learning, and mastery tests for all Sections. These tests enable the teacher to assess student needs before presenting a Section, and to determine any needs for reviewing afterwards.

Basic Skills in English

Book 6 — Recommended for grade 12

Book 5 — Recommended for grade 11

Book 4 — Recommended for grade 10

Book 3 — Recommended for grade 9

Book 2 — Recommended for grade 8

Book 1 — Recommended for grade 7

Basic Skills
in English

BOOK 4

Building Vocabulary

Pages 1–17

Objectives

1. To understand the use of context clues in learning word meanings
2. To gain skill in using inference as a means of understanding words
3. To learn the importance of using synonyms and antonyms
4. To understand the meanings and use of common prefixes
5. To understand the meanings and use of common suffixes
6. To understand the meanings and use of common root words
7. To understand the importance of using sensory words in description

Preparing the Students

Open this section by discussing with students how their own vocabulary has grown since they were toddlers. Encourage them to share recollections of their "baby talk," as well as terms they have acquired recently, such as words for kinds of music, unusual foods, and auto parts. Ask them to reflect on the ways that they have learned new words, such as through conversation, reading, the media, schoolwork. Have them consider the purpose of building their vocabulary further. Explain that each part of Section 1 will help them to gain a wider and more precise vocabulary through the use of context, word analysis, and their senses.

Part 1 **Look for Clues** Learning Word Meanings from Context
pp. 2–3

Objective To understand the use of context clues in learning word meanings

Presenting the Lesson 1. Read aloud *Here's the Idea* and discuss the meaning of the word *context*. Discuss with students the different kinds of context clues: definition, restatement, examples, comparison, and contrast.

2. Read aloud and discuss *Check It Out*. Have students identify each context clue and point out the key words used. (For answers, see Key at back of book.)

3. Assign *Try Your Skill*. Have students underline the key words that they use and write the context clues next to their sentences.

4. Assign *Now Write*. Have students write the context clues next to the words they define. Ask students to share their new words and definitions with the class.

5. An additional challenge is offered in the *Write Again* section of the text, beginning on page 223.

Extending the Lesson Write these nonsense words on the chalkboard: *treep, lunxious, glarky,* and *moonfrous*. Ask students to make up definitions and write sentences that give context clues to the meanings of the words. Afterwards, have each student read a sentence aloud. Let the rest of the class guess the intended definition of the nonsense word.

Part 2 **Take the Hint** Inferring Meaning from Context pp. 4–5

Objective To gain skill in using inference as a means of understanding words

Presenting the Lesson 1. Read aloud and discuss *Here's the Idea*. Read the paragraph containing the word *pandemonium* and point out how, with careful reading, it is not difficult to infer the meaning of many words.

2. Read the paragraph in *Check It Out*. Have students identify key words and expressions that help the reader infer the meaning of *melancholy*. (For answers, see Key at back of book.)

3. Assign and discuss *Try Your Skill*. (For answers, see Key at back of book.)

4. Assign *Now Write*. Allow students to use dictionaries for their sentences about *peace*. Have students share their sentences with the class.

5. See the *Write Again* section of the text, page 223, for an additional writing challenge.

Extending the Lesson Write the following words on the chalkboard:

courage	generosity
beauty	anger
jealousy	sadness
cowardice	sickness
hate	conceit

Have each student select one word and write three or four sentences about a person who possesses that quality. Tell them not to define the word directly. Collect the sentences, read them to the class, and see if everyone can guess the qualities implied.

Part 3 **Say What You Mean** Using Synonyms and Antonyms
pp. 6–7

Objective To learn the importance of using synonyms and antonyms

Presenting the Lesson 1. Before you begin *Here's the Idea*, ask the class if they know the difference between *synonym* and *antonym*. Often students confuse these terms. Sometimes it helps if they can equate *synonym* with *same*; they both begin with the letter *s*. Students can also equate *antonym* with *anti*, meaning "against"; both words begin with the letter *a*.

Read aloud *Here's the Idea* and have students study the synonymy. Tell them that SYN. stands for *synonym* and ANT. stands for *antonym*.

2. Read and discuss *Check It Out*. If students have difficulty answering the first question following the examples, have them refer to the synonymy on page 6. (For answers, see Key.)

3. Assign *Try Your Skill*. Ask students to complete this exercise individually, without the aid of a dictionary; however, if they need to check their work in the dictionary, they may do so. (For answers, see Key.)

4. Assign and discuss *Now Write*.

5. Assign *Write Again*.

Extending the Lesson Divide the class into groups of five and give each group a word that has several synonyms, such as *glad, bright, serious, pity, friend,* or *cruel*. Ask each group to use dictionaries to find five synonyms for the word. Then each student in the group should write a sentence using one of these synonyms. After each group reads its sentences aloud, discuss how the synonyms differ in meaning. Repeat the exercise, using antonyms for the words.

Part 4 **First in Line** Using Prefixes pp. 8–9

Objective To understand the meanings and use of common prefixes

Presenting the Lesson 1. Before you begin the lesson, ask students if they know the meaning of the prefix *pre-*. If they know that *pre-*

means "before," they might not confuse the words *prefix* and *suffix* (which will be discussed in Part 5). Read aloud and discuss *Here's the Idea*. Discuss the list of nine common prefixes. Ask students if they can think of other words containing the prefixes listed.

2. You may have the students complete *Check It Out* orally or write out the answers individually. In either case, make certain that the students know both the prefixes and the base words. (For answers, see Key.)

3. Ask the students to do *Try Your Skill* individually. Do not allow them to confer with each other while finding the three words without prefixes. They may refer to the preceding page in order to find the meanings of the prefixes. (For answers, see Key.)

4. Each student should use his or her own dictionary while completing *Now Write*. If you have an insufficient number of dictionaries, borrow them from classrooms nearby. Have students share the new words with the class.

5. Assign *Write Again*.

Extending the Lesson 1. Review meanings of the nine prefixes. Then hold a definition match, with the same rules as a spelling bee. Ask members of the two teams for definitions of words having the prefixes covered in this part. For a list of words, you might use those generated by students in *Now Write*.

2. Divide the class into teams. Make a game of using dictionaries to find the three prefixes that can be added to each of these base words: *match, heat, enforce, urban, change*. After the new words are announced, instruct students to write definitions.

Part 5 **In Last Place** Using Suffixes   pp. 10–11

Objective To understand the meanings and use of common suffixes

Presenting the Lesson 1. Read aloud *Here's the Idea* and have the students study the list of eight suffixes. Ask students if they can add to the list of examples containing these suffixes.

2. Read the directions for *Check It Out*. You may have students complete this assignment orally or write it individually. (For answers, see Key.)

3. Students may need to refer to dictionaries for the assignment in *Try Your Skill*. Have students complete this assignment individually. Students may also refer to the preceding page for meanings of suffixes. (For answers, see Key.)

4. Read aloud and discuss directions for *Now Write*. Students will need dictionaries for this assignment. Also, students may need to confer with you as to the best definitions for their new words. After everyone has completed the assignment, write some of the new words on the chalkboard. Have students copy these words and their definitions and keep them in their folders.

5. Assign *Write Again*.

Extending the Lesson   Write these pairs of words on the chalkboard:

joyful—joyless   humorist—humorless
restless—restful   odorous—odorless
converter—convertible

Using their knowledge of suffixes, ask students to define these pairs of words formed from the same base words. Have them check definitions in a dictionary and then write a sentence for each word.

Part 6   **Take Root**   Using Roots from Latin   pp. 12–13

Objective   To understand the meanings and use of common root words

Presenting the Lesson   1. Read aloud and discuss *Here's the Idea*. Point out that base words and roots are not necessarily the same. Often a root is not a complete word. Have students study the list of Latin roots on page 12. You may wish to ask your students for additional words that are formed from these Latin roots.

2. *Check It Out* should be a class activity. Write each word on the chalkboard and ask the class to tell you the letters that comprise the Latin root. Underline the root. Discuss how the meaning of the root relates to the meaning of the whole word. (For answers, see Key.)

3. Have students complete *Try Your Skill* individually. Ask the students to avoid using dictionaries if possible. However, if they are uncertain of the meanings or if they have difficulty writing coherent definitions, they should refer to dictionaries. Discuss the Latin roots and the meanings of the words after all students have finished this exercise. (For answers, see Key.)

4. Assign *Now Write*. Write some of the students' new words on the chalkboard and discuss the meanings and the roots. Have students copy the words and their meanings and keep them in their folders. Remind the students that they may not use words already listed in the lesson.

5. Assign *Write Again.*

Extending the Lesson Bring in a newspaper and give each student a page. Ask them to see how many words with Latin roots they can find. Write the words on the chalkboard, underlining the roots. Have students try to figure out the meaning of each word and then check the meanings against the definitions in a dictionary.

Part 7 **It's Sensational!** Building a Vocabulary of the Senses
pp. 14–17

Objective To understand the importance of using sensory words in description

Presenting the Lesson 1. Before reading aloud *Here's the Idea*, discuss the difference between a description that does not use the senses and one that does. Give the students these descriptions: "stopping car," "amazing waves," and "good food." Compare them with the more vivid descriptions in the first paragraph of *Here's the Idea*. Ask students why they need to be aware of their senses when they choose words for descriptions.

2. Read aloud the words in *Check It Out*. If students do not understand some of the words, have them use dictionaries. Review the use of the thesaurus. Show the students that by looking for the word *hit*, for example, they can find synonyms ranging from *poke* to *clobber*. Remind students that although a word may have many synonyms, there is usually only one word that is most effective in a particular context.

3. Read and assign *Try Your Skill.* As students select sensory words to describe the places, they may refer to a thesaurus and to the lists on pages 16 and 17 for additional assistance. After the students have completed this exercise, ask all students who selected "a certain street" to form a group and share their sensory words. Group the rest of your class by the places they chose to describe. Discuss with the entire class how their sensory words differed and how each has created an individual picture.

4. Have students take out a sheet of paper and list four places where they would like to be. Next, have them select one of those places. Discuss and assign *Now Write.*

Extending the Lesson Plan one week filled with activities that will make students more aware of their senses in choosing words. Divide the activities by concentrating on one sense at a time.

1. To make students more aware of visual details, have them examine the photograph on page 30 of the text. Then ask them to close their books and list all the details in the photograph that they can remember. After reading and comparing lists, have students look back at the photograph to see if they can discover new details, such as the displays on the wall or the condition of the basket.

2. Show a variety of photographs from *National Geographic*, *Life* magazine, or a photography book. Have students write their visual impressions. Encourage them to seek exact, precise words such as those listed on page 16.

3. Have all students close their eyes as you bang a pencil against a wastebasket. Then ask them to list words describing the sound. Have them keep their books open to page 16 for examples of hearing words. Instruct students to make more lists as you make the following sounds: crumple paper, scrape chalk on the board, clear your throat, sharpen a pencil.

4. Ask students to choose one of the following scenes to describe to a deaf friend. Remind them to describe sounds precisely.

a horse stable	school halls
a subway	a construction site
a fire	a playground full of children

Discuss the scenes they have created, commenting on vivid sensory words.

5. Review the list of taste words on page 17 before you begin. Give each of four groups of students one of these words: bubble gum, jelly bean, pretzel, raisin. Ask each group to make a list of phrases describing the taste. Then have groups exchange lists, and see if they can add more taste details, such as how the taste and feel change as the item is chewed. Return papers and have volunteers read the lists aloud.

6. Ask students to suggest specific pleasant smells, such as the odor of roses, home-baked cookies, homemade soup, or toast. Choose five, and make columns on the chalkboard. Ask for vivid sensory words to describe each smell. Start with the list on page 17 to see if any words apply. Then ask students for more words of their own. Finally, have students use a thesaurus to find appropriate synonyms. List all these words on the board.

7. Ask students to describe the smells they would expect to find in these places: a basement, a garden, a beauty shop, a gas station, a dry cleaner's, a hospital. Have them use a thesaurus to find new, more precise words. Comment on especially vivid words.

8. Collect five or six objects such as a brush, a Christmas tree ornament, a stapler, a shoe lace, and place each into a separate paper bag. Have students form groups of five and hand a paper bag containing an item to one student in each group. Have that student put his or her hand into the bag and, without telling the item, describe its feeling to the other students in the group. Next, have the other members of the group draw the item on pieces of paper. The paper bags should be passed to different groups with each student taking his or her turn at describing one item to the other members of the group. At the end of this exercise, show the items and discuss some of the words used to describe them.

Improving Your Sentences Pages 19–29

Objectives

1. To identify and use clear, interesting sentences
2. To include only related details in sentences
3. To avoid writing sentences that are repetitive or that state unsupported opinions
4. To avoid sentences padded with useless words
5. To avoid overloading sentences with too many ideas

Preparing the Students

Write the following groups of words on the chalkboard:

    1. a large woman with a large purse she
    2. was that had everything in it
    3. but a hammer and nails

Ask students why the groups of words do not make sense. Then instruct them to write one complete sentence using all the words in the three fragments. ("She was a large woman with a large purse that had everything in it but a hammer and nails."—LANGSTON HUGHES) Compare the fuzziness of the fragments with the clarity of the composite sentence.

As they begin this section on sentences, remind students of the following:

1. Sentences contain subjects and predicates and express complete thoughts. (See page 259 of the Handbook for review.)

2. Well written sentences convey meaning clearly and directly.

Tell students that this section will help them to write precise, clear sentences.

Part 1 **Power Play** Using Sentences   pp. 20–21

Objective To identify and use clear, interesting sentences

Presenting the Lesson 1. Read aloud *Here's the Idea.* Emphasize the definition of *sentence.* Ask what makes each of the sample sentences powerful.

2. Discuss *Check It Out.* Write the first sentence on the chalkboard, leaving out the word *raced:* "Neil _____ up the path after his friend." Have students supply different verbs to see how the meaning of the sentence changes. Point out how word choice helps make these sentences vivid.

3. Assign and discuss *Try Your Skill.* Remind students that a sentence is a complete thought. Encourage students to revise their sentences until they are clear and direct.

4. Assign *Now Write.* Have students brainstorm in order to find three original topics for their sentences. For example, ask students to think about the two most important things in their lives. After they have written original sentences, encourage students to revise their sentences for clarity.

Extending the Lesson Have the students write the names of five of their favorite television shows, past or present. Then have the students select only one of these shows to describe in one sentence. Instruct them to make specific statements that will distinguish the TV show from all others. Have students read their sentences aloud, without saying the title of the show. See if the other students can identify the show.

2. Copy the following chart on the chalkboard:

Dull	Vivid
I saw the fireworks.	Fireworks streaked across the
There was a bullfight.	night sky.
This music is good.	At bullfights, young men taunt
I ate a lot.	bulls in the ring.

Ask students what makes the sentences in the left-hand column dull and those in the right-hand column vivid. Have them try to fill in the right-hand column for the last two sentences. Ask volunteers to read their sentences aloud.

Part 2 **Stay with It** Keeping to the Point   pp. 22–23

Objective To include only related details in sentences

Presenting the Lesson 1. Read aloud and discuss *Here's the Idea*. Point out the three sentences beginning with the word *Frank*. Discuss their differences. Read the sentences beginning with the words *In Washington*. Contrast related and unrelated details.

2. Discuss *Check It Out*. (For answers, see Key at back of book.) Have students point out the unrelated details. Ask for interesting related details that might be added.

3. Assign and discuss *Try Your Skill*. (For answers, see Key at back of book.) Have volunteers share their revisions with the class.

4. Assign *Now Write*. It may be difficult for the students to find examples of sentences that do not keep to the point. You might suggest that the students review their own writing contained in their folders. Another possibility is to suggest that students write two sentences about a state or city they have visited. Then they should add related details to make the sentences clear and interesting.

Extending the Lesson Distribute copies of these sentences to your students:

1. Luis piled three scoops of ice cream on top of the banana slices. Luis works part-time.

2. Jeanne took the subway to Wilson Stadium. The game between the Phillies and the Cardinals was being played at Wilson Stadium.

3. Some people like TV commercials better than TV programs. Commercials are usually either thirty or sixty seconds long.

4. Melinda ran in the women's marathon. Melinda was pleased that she had finished the race.

Discuss which pairs of sentences have related ideas. Ask students to combine the sentences with related ideas into single sentences. Discuss which pairs of sentences contain unrelated ideas. Have students make up a related idea to add to each of the sentences.

Part 3 **Nothing Doing** Avoiding Empty Sentences pp. 24–25

Objective To avoid writing sentences that are repetitive or that have unsupported opinions

Presenting the Lesson 1. Read aloud and discuss *Here's the Idea*. Differentiate between the empty sentence that states the same idea twice and the empty sentence that gives an unsupported opinion.

2. Divide the class into groups of three to discuss *Check It Out*. Have the groups revise the sentences. (For answers, see Key.) Ask one student from each group to read that group's improved sentences. Comment on details used.

3. Assign and discuss *Try Your Skill*. (For answers, see Key.) Have volunteers share their revisions with the class. Point out the specific ideas that the revised sentences contain.

4. Assign *Now Write*. Ask the students to bring to class two examples of each kind of empty sentence. If they cannot find examples in newspapers or magazines, you may suggest that they write their own sentences about the following topics: a favorite car design, a favorite TV star, a favorite sport, a vacation, a good friend. Stress that each sentence should be revised carefully.

Extending the Lesson Pair students to take turns interviewing each other. Have them ask these questions:

1. What is your opinion of pro football?
2. What kind of job would you like to have?
3. What kind of friend are you?
4. How do you feel about disco music?
5. What do you think of sports cars?

Instruct them to write each other's responses in sentence form and to place a check mark in front of any repetitive statement or unsupported opinion. Have the partners exchange papers. Ask them to rewrite any empty sentences.

Objective To avoid sentences padded with useless words

Presenting the Lesson 1. Read aloud *Here's the Idea*. Review the common phrases used for padding on page 26. Ask the students why these phrases are used frequently. Stress that they are unacceptable in writing even though they are common in speaking. As you read the examples of padded sentences and the improved sentences, point out how the improved sentences express the same idea more concisely.

2. Discuss *Check It Out*. (For answers, see Key.) Ask students to explain what is wrong with each sentence and how it can be improved.

3. Assign and discuss *Try Your Skill*. (For answers, see Key.) Have volunteers share their improved sentences with the class.

4. Read aloud the directions for *Now Write*. Specifically tell your students to be aware of the words *you know*. Then have them listen for padded sentences used at the lunch table, in classes, at work, or at home. If they do not find examples of padded sentences, they may create four examples of their own to revise.

Extending the Lesson Divide the class into groups of five. Give each group one sentence from a newspaper editorial. Ask each member of the group to add a different phrase from page 26 or to add a padded phrase of their own to the sentence. Have each group exchange the sentences they have written with another group. Ask groups to discuss how the sentences should be revised.

Part 5 **In Short** Avoiding Overloaded Sentences   pp. 28–29

Objective To avoid overloading sentences with too many ideas

Presenting the Lesson 1. Read aloud *Here's the Idea*. In the first example, ask students how many *and's* were used. Ask which *and's* connect unrelated thoughts. Point out the changes made in the revision.

2. Discuss *Check It Out*. Point out the words used to begin the sentences in the revision.

3. Assign and discuss *Try Your Skill*. (For answers, see Key.) Allow students to use only one *and* in each of the three sentences.

13

4. Assign *Now Write*. First, have students check their own folders containing past writings. If they find overloaded sentences, they may revise these sentences. If they do not find overloaded sentences, they may create four examples to revise.

Extending the Lesson 1. Copy the following passage on the chalkboard. Tell students that you have altered a passage from a short story by Isaac Bashevis Singer to make overloaded sentences. Ask them to revise the paragraph.

> Somewhere, sometime, there lived a rich man whose name was Kadish, and he had an only son who was called Atzel, and in the household of Kadish there lived a distant relative, an orphan girl, called Aksah, and Atzel was a tall boy with black hair and black eyes, and Aksah was somewhat shorter than Atzel, and she had blue eyes and golden hair, and both were about the same age, and as children, they ate together, studied together, played together, and Atzel played the husband; Aksah, his wife, and it was taken for granted that when they grew up they would really marry.

Have the students share their revisions. You might read aloud the actual passage:

> Somewhere, sometime, there lived a rich man whose name was Kadish. He had an only son who was called Atzel. In the household of Kadish there lived a distant relative, an orphan girl, called Aksah. Atzel was a tall boy with black hair and black eyes. Aksah was somewhat shorter than Atzel, and she had blue eyes and golden hair. Both were about the same age. As children, they ate together, studied together, played together. Atzel played the husband; Aksah, his wife. It was taken for granted that when they grew up they would really marry.

2. Have students begin by writing one sentence about something that they remember from grade school. Then have all students pass their papers to their right. Ask each student to add *and* or *but* and to continue the story with another sentence. Rotate two more times. Then ask students to rewrite the overloaded sentences that have been created. Have volunteers read "befores" and "afters" aloud.

What Is a Paragraph?

Objectives

1. To understand that a paragraph is a group of sentences dealing with one main idea
2. To recognize and write unified paragraphs
3. To recognize and write topic sentences of paragraphs
4. To identify and use three kinds of paragraph development
5. To identify the three kinds of paragraphs: narrative, descriptive, and explanatory

Preparing the Students

Read the following passage to your students:

> The lieutenant looked up. He had a face that once had been brown and now the rain had washed it pale. The rain had washed the color from his eyes and they were white, as were his teeth, and as was his hair. He was all white. Even his uniform was beginning to turn white, and perhaps a little green with fungus.—RAY BRADBURY

Ask students what picture the passage conveys to them. Ask them what feeling they get from the passage. Point out that in paragraphs like the one just read, single sentences work together for a certain purpose. Tell students that in this section they will learn how sentences combine to form paragraphs.

Part 1 **An Idea at Work** Defining a Paragraph pp. 32–33

Objective To understand that a paragraph is a group of sentences dealing with one main idea

Presenting the Lesson 1. Read aloud and discuss *Here's the Idea*. Emphasize the definition of *paragraph*. Read each of the three paragraphs to the class. Then have the students read each one silently. Ask them what main idea connects all the sentences in each paragraph. Discuss how each sentence contributes to the main idea.
2. Discuss *Check It Out*.

3. Assign *Try Your Skill*. Divide the class into groups of three. Have the groups decide which group of sentences is a paragraph and state its main idea. Encourage the groups to explain their answers to the rest of the class. If there is disagreement among the students, refer them to the definition of a paragraph.

4. Assign *Now Write*.

Extending the Lesson Hand out current magazines such as *Sports Illustrated, Seventeen,* and *Car and Driver.* Have each student randomly select a paragraph and check to see that it deals with one main idea. Then ask students to write down the main idea and note how each sentence supports that idea. Have students read their paragraphs to the class and share their conclusions.

Part 2 **With One Voice** Recognizing Unity in a Paragraph
pp. 34–35

Objective To recognize and write unified paragraphs

Presenting the Lesson 1. Read aloud and discuss *Here's the Idea.* Ask students to state the main idea of the Volcano Sundae paragraph. Point out how each sentence relates to the main idea.

2. Discuss *Check It Out.* Ask how each sentence relates to the main idea. Point out that whether a paragraph explains, tells a story, or describes, it should be unified by one main idea.

3. Assign and discuss *Try Your Skill.* (For answers, see Key.) After the students copy the main idea on their papers, ask them what the key words are in the main idea. Remind them that if a sentence does not relate to either "mysterious" or "unusual place," the sentence does not belong in that paragraph. Have students compare their answers.

4. Assign *Now Write.* Have students brainstorm by listing places they know well: home, work, a vacation spot, school cafeteria. Have the students select only one of the ideas from their lists. Then they may continue the assignment. After students have written the sentences, instruct them to make sure that the sentences all deal with the same main idea.

Extending the Lesson 1. Assign students to work in pairs. Tell each student to write a sentence answering this question: Would you rather live in the city, the suburbs, or the country? Ask them to write five sentences explaining their choices with specific reasons. Then have partners exchange papers and check that all sentences are related to the main idea. Partners should cross out unrelated sentences and substitute related ones.

2. Make copies of the following paragraph and distribute them to the students. Do not underline the two unrelated sentences.

> An abrupt sound startled him. Off to the right he heard it, and his ears, expert in such matters, could not be mistaken. Again he heard the sound, and again. *He enjoyed music of all kinds.* Somewhere, off in the blackness, someone had fired a gun three times. *In Westerns, cowboys always ride horses and have gunfights.*—RICHARD CONNELL

Ask students if the paragraph is unified. Have them cross out any unrelated sentences and write the main idea of the paragraph.

Part 3 **In Control** Using a Topic Sentence pp. 36–37

Objective To recognize and write topic sentences of paragraphs

Presenting the Lesson 1. Read aloud and discuss *Here's the Idea.* Emphasize the definition of a *topic sentence.* Point out that a topic sentence has three important functions in a paragraph. For examples of topic sentences, you might refer to page 34 and discuss the first sentence in each of the three sample paragraphs.

2. Discuss *Check It Out.* Ask for a show of hands to see if the students can identify which sentence is the topic sentence. Point out how all the other sentences relate to the topic sentence.

3. Read the instructions for *Try Your Skill.* (For answers, see Key.) Read each paragraph twice for the class. Then give the students time to write the topic sentence for each paragraph. Discuss their answers. If there are disagreements, remind students that all the other sentences should support the topic sentence.

4. Assign *Now Write.* If the students have difficulty thinking of topics, suggest that they state what they like to do on holidays, what their favorite pet is, or how to make their favorite foods. Remind them that their topic sentence can describe, explain, or tell a story.

Extending the Lesson Distribute copies of a short newspaper editorial on a current topic of interest. After you have read the editorial aloud, ask students to underline the topic sentence in each paragraph. Have students share their answers.

What a Buildup! Ways of Developing a Paragraph
pp. 38–39

Objective To identify and use three kinds of paragraph development

Presenting the Lesson 1. Read aloud the first paragraph in *Here's the Idea.* Explain that details are "specifics" that make a subject come alive. Read aloud the paragraph using details. Ask the class to identify the details, and also the topic sentence. Next, read the paragraph using examples. Ask what the topic sentence is and what example is used in this paragraph. Finally, read aloud the paragraph using facts and figures. Have the students name the topic sentence and the facts and figures used to support the first sentence. Review by identifying the topic sentence and the method of development in each paragraph.

2. Discuss *Check It Out.* Ask students to identify the topic sentence. Ask which words and phrases support the topic sentence. If the students have difficulty discerning between examples and facts and figures, refer to the paragraphs on the preceding page.

3. Assign and discuss *Try Your Skill.* Compare this paragraph with the one using details on the preceding page.

4. Assign *Now Write.* Read the directions and note that they call for only three details, three examples, or three facts and figures. Students should not combine details, examples, and facts and figures at this time.

Extending the Lesson 1. Select articles from a few weekly magazines. Ask students to locate paragraphs that are clearly developed by either details, examples, or facts and figures. Have volunteers read their paragraphs and identify the topic sentence and method of development.

2. Extend the *Write Again* activity. Ask your students to choose one of the topic sentences. Then ask them to write three sentences to develop that topic sentence with facts and figures, examples, or details.

3. Have students turn back to the paragraphs on pages 32, 34, and 37. Ask them to identify the way that each paragraph is developed.

Part 5 **Nameplates** Recognizing Three Kinds of Paragraphs
pp. 40–41

Objective To identify the three kinds of paragraphs: narrative, descriptive, and explanatory

Presenting the Lesson 1. Read aloud *Here's the Idea.* Emphasize the definitions of narrative, descriptive, and explanatory paragraphs. Ask the class to give examples of times when they have used these three kinds of paragraphs in their writing. Perhaps they have written funny stories about themselves. Perhaps they have written descriptions of their homes. Perhaps they have written directions for how to assemble things or how to play games.

2. Discuss *Check It Out.* Point out that the three paragraphs deal with the same topic in three different ways. Ask students what the purpose of each paragraph is and what makes the first paragraph narrative, the second one descriptive, and the third one explanatory.

3. Assign and discuss *Try Your Skill.* Encourage students to defend their answers and convince others who disagree with them. If students do not agree that the paragraph is explanatory, review the definitions on page 40.

4. Assign *Now Write.*

Extending the Lesson 1. Divide the class into three groups. Make each group responsible for one type of paragraph: narrative, descriptive, or explanatory. Have the groups look through their other textbooks to find at least three examples of their assigned type of paragraph. Ask each group to share these paragraphs with the rest of the class.

2. Copy this list on the chalkboard:

handbook on plant care	encyclopedia article
front-page newspaper story	cookbook
travel brochure	sports story
biology textbook	letter from a friend
short story	school newspaper editorial

Ask students which of these would be likely sources for narrative paragraphs and have them explain why. Ask which would be probable sources of descriptive paragraphs and have students tell why. Ask which would be likely sources for explanatory paragraphs and why. Point out that each of the above sources could have different types of paragraphs.

3. Have students turn to the paragraphs on pages 32, 34, 36, 37, 38, and 39. Ask students to identify each as narrative, descriptive, or explanatory.

4. Give your students the following topic sentence: The rocket shot off in a burst of flames. Ask one-third of the students to write three sentences supporting the topic sentence as part of a descriptive

paragraph. Ask one-third of the students to write three sentences for a narrative paragraph and the rest to write three sentences for an explanatory paragraph. After you collect the papers, read representative examples.

Writing a Paragraph Pages 43–51

Objectives

1. To acquire the skill of limiting the topic for a paragraph
2. To write direct, lively topic sentences
3. To learn to develop paragraphs by using details, examples, or facts and figures
4. To end a paragraph with an interesting sentence that sums up the main idea

Preparing the Students

Have the students take out a blank sheet of paper. Tell students that you are going to experiment with them. Tell them that you are going to give them a subject to write about for five minutes. Stress that they should write whatever comes into their minds and should not take their pencils or pens off their papers. Mention that you will not be grading these papers. Tell them not to worry about misspellings or punctuation. When all students are ready to write, give them this topic: machines.

After the students have written for five minutes, ask them to look back at what they have written. Ask how they dealt with the topic and how they felt about writing in this way.

Ask the students if they think their writing is organized. Ask if their writing is easy to follow.

Point out that effective paragraphs need to be planned in advance. Tell them that this section will teach them skills for planning and writing paragraphs of their own.

Objective   To acquire the skill of limiting the topic for a paragraph

Presenting the Lesson   1. Read aloud *Here's the Idea*. Stress the importance of asking questions in order to find the specifics for a topic. Read the paragraph on page 44. Point out how the *who, what, when, where, why,* and *how* questions are used to narrow the original topic, music.

2. Read aloud and discuss *Check It Out*. Tell students that the more specifically they answer the six questions, the more detailed and interesting their paragraphs will be.

3. Read the instructions for *Try Your Skill*. Have students write a list of questions at the left side of their papers and answer the questions with specific details at the right side of their papers.

4. Assign *Now Write*. You may suggest that the students select two of the four other general topics found in *Try Your Skill*.

Extending the Lesson   Select three or four one-paragraph articles from the "People" section of *Time* magazine. Duplicate them and give copies to your students. For each paragraph, have students explain how the following questions are answered: *who, what, when, where, why,* and *how*. Mention that not all of the questions will be answered in every paragraph.

Objective   To write direct, lively topic sentences

Presenting the Lesson   1. Read aloud and discuss *Here's the Idea*. Emphasize that in addition to stating the main idea clearly, a topic sentence should be direct and lively.

2. Read and discuss *Check It Out*. Ask students if the topic sentences could be made more direct and lively.

3. Assign *Try Your Skill* to groups of three students. Have each group revise all four sentences. These sentence revisions may be shared with the rest of the class.

4. Assign *Now Write*. Remind students that they will be using these topic sentences at a later date.

Extending the Lesson   Write the following topics on the board:

1. Blue jeans
2. Three-speed bicycles
3. Free agents in baseball or football
4. Movie ratings (such as PG and R)

Have each student choose one of these four topics and write a direct, lively topic sentence about it. Collect the sentences and read them to the class. Point out the variety of viewpoints in these sentences. Have the class select the two best sentences for each of the four topics.

Part 3   **Deliver the Goods**   How To Develop a Paragraph
pp. 48–49

Objective   To learn to develop paragraphs by using details, examples, or facts and figures

Presenting the Lesson   1. Before reading *Here's the Idea*, you might have the class first review page 38 for the three ways to develop paragraphs.

2. Read and discuss the paragraph in *Check It Out*. First, have students identify the topic sentence. Then have students count how many facts and figures are used to develop the topic sentence.

3. Assign *Try Your Skill*. Ask each student to write each topic sentence on a sheet of paper. Then they should write either *details*, *examples*, or *facts and figures* below the topic sentence. Have students discuss and defend their answers.

4. Assign *Now Write*. After the students complete their paragraphs, ask them to exchange papers with a partner. The partner should comment if a better topic sentence or more specific development is needed.

Extending the Lesson   Have students revise or use one of the topic sentences written for *Extending the Lesson*, Section 4, Part 2. Ask students to write complete paragraphs, using details, examples, or facts and figures. Collect them and read some examples of effective paragraphs to the class.

Part 4   **A Big Finish**   How To Write a Good Ending   pp. 50–51

Objective   To end a paragraph with an interesting sentence that sums up the main idea

Presenting the Lesson 1. Read aloud and discuss *Here's the Idea*. It is very important that your class understand the third sentence. Emphasize that a good ending sentence ties the ideas of the paragraph together.

2. Read and discuss *Check It Out*. Have the class answer the two questions about the sample paragraph. For an additional example of an effective ending sentence, have the class read the Double Eagle II paragraph on page 48.

3. Assign and discuss *Try Your Skill*. If your students have difficulty, read these paragraphs to the class. If the students still cannot think of concluding sentences, pair each student with a partner. Ask both to brainstorm and to write concluding sentences together.

4. Assign *Now Write*. Have students use the paragraphs assigned on page 49.

Extending the Lesson 1. Distribute this paragraph to students or write it on the chalkboard:

> On the first warm day of spring, people gather to enjoy the weather together. Beaches that have been empty all winter are suddenly jammed with sun-seekers. Newly green parks come alive with children's laughing and shouting. The hum of bikes and roller-skates, and the buzzing of motorcycles invades the quiet landscape.

Ask your students to provide an ending sentence that will tie the paragraph together in an interesting way. Have volunteers read their sentences aloud, and comment on strong sentences.

2. Collect the paragraphs completed in the *Now Write* activity. Compile these paragraphs into a mini-newspaper with a title such as "Views in the News." Duplicate the newspaper and give students time to look it over. Then ask them to point out well narrowed topics, good topic sentences, especially effective paragraph development, and lively ending sentences.

A Writer's Choices

Objectives

1. To understand the literary definition of *point of view*
2. To recognize and use first-person point of view
3. To recognize and use third-person point of view and omniscient point of view
4. To understand the difference between nonfiction and fiction
5. To use accurate facts when writing nonfiction and specific details when writing fiction
6. To learn how to choose specific verbs and adjectives to create mood
7. To identify and write interesting titles

Preparing the Students

Ask your students to suggest a food that they all have prepared, such as scrambled eggs or a sandwich. Then, on the chalkboard, jot down the choices they make during that process, such as what ingredients to use and how to combine them. Compare that process with the process of writing, noting that choices are made at each step. Point out that in both writing and cooking, the choices that are made affect how good the final product is.

Ask students to review the writer's choices they have studied so far. They include narrowing the topic, choosing a topic sentence, deciding how to develop the topic sentence, and selecting a good ending sentence. Tell your students that in this section they will learn about more choices that a writer must make.

Part 1   **I Say!**   How To Use a Personal Point of View   **pp. 54–55**

Objectives   1. To understand the literary definition of *point of view*
2. To recognize and use first-person point of view

Presenting the Lesson   1. Before reading *Here's the Idea,* ask students what the difference is between these two sentences:

24

It was raining so hard that my sister and I could barely see the street as we drove to the hospital.

The two girls drove through heavy rains to the hospital.

Emphasize that the main difference is in the point of view used in each. The first sentence is told from the view of the person experiencing the action. The second is from the point of view of someone observing the action. Read aloud and discuss *Here's the Idea,* emphasizing the definitions of *point of view* and first-person point of view. Have students check their folders to see if any of their paragraphs use first-person point of view.

2. Read and discuss *Check It Out.* Ask students why they think the authors of these paragraphs used first-person point of view.

3. Read aloud the directions for *Try Your Skill.* Have students read both paragraphs silently and rewrite the incorrect sentences. Ask why the sentences must be changed. Have volunteers read their revisions.

4. Assign *Now Write.* Have the class brainstorm for ideas. Ask students to write the names of four imaginary characters taken from newspaper comic strips, television, or cartoons. You might suggest literary characters such as Scrooge or Tom Sawyer. Ask the students to select one character and follow the instructions.

Extending the Lesson   1. Have each student write a paragraph about an embarrassing moment. The paragraphs should be written from the first-person point of view. Have volunteers share their paragraphs with others in the class.

2. Display three or four magazine photographs picturing athletics or adventure. Instruct students to suppose that they are one of the people in the photograph and that they are describing what is happening. Ask them to write a paragraph using first-person point of view.

Part 2   **In the Know**   How To Use an Outsider's Point of View
pp. 56–57

Objective   To recognize and use third-person point of view and omniscient point of view

Presenting the Lesson   1. Read aloud and discuss *Here's the Idea.* Discuss omniscient point of view. Point out that the prefix *omni-* means "all." Ask students what omniscient point of view allows writers to do. Review the difference between omniscient and third-person points of view.

Put the following chart on the chalkboard without filling in the pronouns. Ask students what pronouns they would use to refer to characters described from each point of view. Fill in the chart. Have students copy it and keep it in their folders.

First Person	Third Person	Omniscient
I	he, she, it, they	he, she, it, they
me	him, her, it, them	him, her, it, them
my, mine	his, hers, its, their, theirs	his, hers, its, their, theirs

2. Read and discuss *Check It Out*. Ask students why they think Gina Berriault chose third-person point of view and why Jack London chose omniscient point of view in these particular paragraphs.

3. Assign *Try Your Skill* to groups of three. Then have the groups state the point of view of the paragraph and the reasons for their decisions.

4. Assign *Now Write*. You might have students select characters from the lists they made for Part 1.

Extending the Lesson 1. Give your students this situation:

A landlord is telling a woman and her four-year-old child that they must move out of their apartment immediately because they haven't paid the rent.

Divide the class into four groups. Ask the students in each group to write narrative paragraphs based on this situation. Assign each group one of these points of view: first person with the landlord as narrator, first person with the woman as narrator, first person with the child as narrator, third person omniscient. After the paragraphs are finished, have the students in each group share their writing and decide on one paragraph to read aloud to the class. Discuss the differences in the situations that point of view makes.

2. Have students imagine that they are telling about a Martian landing during halftime at the Super Bowl. Ask them first to write one paragraph telling about the landing from the third-person point of view. Then ask them to adapt the paragraph to make it omniscient point of view. Remind your students that the second paragraph should note the reactions and feelings of the Martians as well as those of the football crowd.

Objectives 1. To understand the differences between nonfiction and fiction

2. To use accurate facts when writing nonfiction and specific details when writing fiction

Presenting the Lesson 1. Read aloud *Here's the Idea.* Discuss the differences between nonfiction and fiction. You might use television news reporting as an example of nonfiction and a story about Superman as an example of fiction.

2. Read aloud and discuss *Check It Out.* Ask your students which facts are used in the first paragraph and which details are used to build the second paragraph.

3. Assign and discuss *Try Your Skill.* Point out that the first part of this exercise will be non-fiction, while the second part of the exercise will be fiction.

4. Assign *Now Write.* Have students refer to page 40 if they need to review the three kinds of paragraphs. Assist your students by writing the following on the chalkboard:

> Choose a topic.
> Narrow the topic.
> List either facts or details.
> Decide on the kind of paragraph.
> Decide on first-person or third-person point of view.
> Write a first draft.
> Revise.
> Write a final draft.

Extending the Lesson 1. Have students write four or five facts about themselves. The facts might include famous ancestors, cities where they have lived, or family members. Then have students create unusual fictitious details about themselves. Ask students to write one first-person paragraph using either the facts or the imaginary details.

2. Distribute a newspaper article and a short story to students in your class. Have them select one paragraph from the newspaper article and list all the facts it contains. Then have them choose one paragraph from the short story and list all the imaginary details it contains.

Objective To learn how to choose specific verbs and adjectives to create moods

Presenting the Lesson 1. Read aloud and discuss *Here's the Idea*. If your students have difficulty identifying verbs and adjectives, refer to Handbook Sections 5 and 6.

2. Read and discuss *Check It Out*. As a class activity, have the students point out the strong, specific words. List them on the chalkboard.

3. Read aloud and discuss *Try Your Skill*. Have students point out the weak verbs and adjectives. Then have them form groups of three to revise the paragraph. Ask volunteers to read the new paragraphs aloud.

4. Assign *Now Write*. Encourage students to use a thesaurus or a dictionary.

Extending the Lesson 1. Divide the class into teams for this game. Give the teams five minutes to write all the strong words they can think of to replace the word *said*, such as *shout, cry,* and *stammer*. See which team can think of the most words, and have that team read its words aloud. You may repeat this activity using these words: *walk, look, large, happy, old, pretty, say, small*. For some of the words, allow the groups to use a thesaurus.

2. On the chalkboard, write these examples of synonyms that create different feelings:

I am *plump*.	You are *heavy*.	He is *fat*.
I am *strict*.	You are *stern*.	She is *mean*.
I am active.	You are _____.	He is _____.
I am _____.	You are _____.	She is *lazy*.

As a class, finish the last two, and then have individual students write two more sets of their own. Ask volunteers to read these aloud.

Part 5 **Namedropping** How To Write a Good Title   pp. **62–63**

Objective To identify and use interesting titles

Presenting the Lesson 1. Read aloud and discuss *Here's the Idea*. Ask students if the title of a book or article has ever caught their attention. Have your students scan the first five sections of their English textbooks for the titles. They might note that each chapter has not only a main title, but also a more specific subtitle.

2. Read and discuss the titles listed in *Check It Out*. Then have students use their imaginations by guessing what these stories might be about.

3. Assign and discuss *Try Your Skill*. Have students share their best titles with the class.

4. Assign *Now Write*. These titles might also be shared.

Extending the Lesson 1. Take your class to the school library to look for twenty interesting and creative book titles. Students should write the titles and the subject matter of these books. The titles can be shared with the class at a later date.

2. Bring a TV guide to class. Mention the names of various television programs. Ask students to comment on especially good titles. Then have each student make up titles for three imaginary television programs.

3. Divide the class into groups of four. Have each group devise a "Title Checklist." It should ask questions that a writer should consider when writing a title. Suggest this example for one of the checklist items:

_____ Does the title suggest the main idea of the piece of writing?

After the checklists are finished and have been approved by you, tell students to keep the checklists in their folders to refer to when they write.

The Process of Writing   Pages 65–69

Objectives

1. To understand that pre-writing involves narrowing the topic, deciding on a point of view, and making notes
2. To learn how to write a first draft
3. To learn to revise, rewrite, and proofread a piece of writing

Preparing the Students

Write the following headings on the chalkboard: *Before, During,* and *After.* Tell your students that these headings refer to the writing process. Have your students place the following activities under these headings:

Deciding on a point of view	Listing possible topics
Proofreading	Choosing a topic
Listing details	Making a final copy
Writing a rough draft	Creating titles
Constructing sentences	Examining the writing
Replacing weak words	Checking capitalization and
Reorganizing ideas	punctuation
Narrowing the topic	Deciding the kind of
	paragraph

Most likely, they will see that these activities are appropriate at different times in the process of writing. Leave the categories on the board as you begin Section 6. Tell students that in Section 6 they will see what is involved at each stage of the writing process.

Presenting the Lesson 1. Read aloud and discuss *Before You Write.* Be sure that the following activities are under the word *Before* on the chalkboard:

Listing possible topics
Choosing a topic
Narrowing the topic
Deciding on a point of view
Listing details
Deciding the kind of paragraph

Have the students study the sample pre-writing exercise on page 67.

2. Read aloud *When You Write.* Stress that in the first draft the writing need not be perfect. Be sure you have listed the following categories under the word *During* on the chalkboard:

Constructing sentences
Writing a rough draft

Add this to the list:

Ignoring organization and mechanics

3. Read aloud and discuss *After You Write.* Make sure you have listed the following activities under the word *After* on the chalkboard:

Examining the writing for interesting and clear ideas
Reorganizing ideas
Replacing weak words
Checking capitalization and punctuation
Writing an effective title
Making a final copy
Proofreading

Make certain that students study the example illustrated on page 68 and the final draft on page 69. Ask them why each change was made. Review the steps in the writing process.

As a summary of this section, stress that you can learn to write only by writing.

Extending the Lesson 1. Have students copy the list on the chalkboard to keep for handy reference whenever they write.

2. Stimulate interest in the writing process by posting interesting newspaper articles, humorous tidbits, thought-provoking sayings, and unique cartoons on the bulletin board. You may also want to encourage your students to keep journals, recording their impressions of events, places, and people. You might set aside a few minutes at the end of each class period for journal writing. Tell your students that the details recorded in a journal can provide subject matter for later writing.

The Narrative Paragraph Pages 71–77

Objectives

1. To recognize and use chronological order in narrative paragraphs

2. To use details in developing narrative paragraphs

3. To gain skill in using transitions to show chronological order

Preparing the Students

Ask students to tell what happened in a movie or TV show they have seen recently. After their comments, point out that the students not only told narratives but also told the events in the order that they occurred. Review the definition of a narrative paragraph. Tell students that Section 7 will show them how to write good narrative paragraphs.

Part 1 **What Happens Next?** How To Use Chronological Order
pp. 72–73

Objective To recognize and use chronological order in narrative paragraphs

Presenting the Lesson 1. Read aloud *Here's the Idea*. Write the word *chronological*, along with its definition, on the chalkboard. Read Peter Abrahams's paragraph and point out the step-by-step order of the narrative. Note, too, that the narrative begins with a strong sentence.

You might have your students refer to the first example on page 40 for another good narrative paragraph.

2. Read and discuss John Steinbeck's paragraph in *Check It Out*. Have the class summarize the events in chronological order.

3. Read aloud the directions for *Try Your Skill*. (For answers, see Key.) Have students complete this assignment and compare answers. Ask one student to read the events in chronological order.

4. Assign *Now Write*. Remind the class of the steps in *The Process of Writing* (Section 6). If students need ideas for those paragraphs, suggest that they think of a humorous experience they have had lately.

Extending the Lesson Divide the class into groups of three. Have the groups put these sentences in chronological order and then write a strong opening sentence for the paragraph:

1. Although we searched the apartment and the entire neighborhood, we couldn't find Waffles, so we had to leave without him.

2. Then we labeled each carton.

3. To our surprise, from out of the carton marked *food* jumped Waffles.

4. When we arrived at our new apartment, we unpacked the cartons.

5. On moving day we packed all of our belongings into huge cartons.

6. After we had loaded all the cartons onto the van, we noticed that our dog Waffles was missing.

When the groups have finished, ask one student to read the sentences in chronological order. Ask for volunteers to read sample opening sentences.

Part 2 **Any Questions?** How To Develop a Narrative Paragraph
pp. 74–75

Objective To use details in developing narrative paragraphs

Presenting the Lesson 1. Before you read *Here's the Idea*, have the class refer to page 44. Reread the narrative paragraph using details. Emphasize that although all six questions are not needed for every topic, they can help writers get down to specifics.
2. Read aloud and discuss *Check It Out*. Point out that this paragraph is written from the first-person point of view. Show students that the paragraph has good beginning and concluding sentences. Ask the class to pick out the details by asking the six questions discussed earlier.
3. Read aloud the directions for *Try Your Skill*. You might stimulate a pre-writing discussion by telling of a frightening experience you have had, or ask students to do the same. Have students list the six questions at the left-hand sides of their papers and specific details at the right.
4. Assign *Now Write*. Students may use the incidents related in *Try Your Skill*, or they may use the six questions to think of details for a new story. They should also follow *The Process of Writing* outlined in Section 6. If you collect the paragraphs, you might want to read the ten best ones to the class.

Extending the Lesson 1. Have students look at copies of your school newspaper. You can probably obtain old copies from the journalism teacher at your school. Have each student take a different news article and see if the first paragraph answers all six questions. Point out that good news articles usually answer *who, what, when, where, how,* and *why* early in the story. Ask students to share their conclusions with the rest of the class.
2. Distribute this paragraph and read it aloud to your students:

Across the sky, very high and beautiful, a rocket burned on a sweep of orange fire. It circled and came down, causing all to gasp. It landed, setting the meadow afire here and there. The fire burned out, the rocket lay a moment in quiet, and then, as the silent crowd watched, a great door in the side of the vessel whispered out a breath of oxygen. The door slid back, and an old man stepped out.—RAY BRADBURY

Ask students if the six questions are answered in this paragraph and how they are answered. Within the paragraph, have them underline details that they think are especially vivid. Let students discuss their responses.

3. Ask students to observe a sports event and then write a narrative paragraph summarizing the game or meet. Remind them to include vivid details.

Part 3 **Time Will Tell** How To Use Transitions in a Narrative
pp. 76–77

Objective To gain skill in using transitions to show chronological order

Presenting the Lesson 1. Read aloud *Here's the Idea.* Emphasize the definition of *transitions.* Have students copy the list of transitions to keep in their folders for referral. They may label their papers *Transitions in a Narrative.*

2. Read aloud and discuss *Check It Out.* Emphasize that the function of transitions in a narrative is to show chronological order. As students find transitions, list them on the chalkboard. Point out that Woody Guthrie used his different ages to show the passing of time.

3. Assign and discuss *Try Your Skill.* Remind students to choose a variety of transitions. After students finish rewriting the paragraph, ask them to share their revisions with others. If students chose different periods of time, comment on the options that writers have.

4. Assign *Now Write.* Refer students to the list of transitions on page 76 as well as Section 6, *The Process of Writing.*

Extending the Lesson 1. Ask students to take out their paragraphs written for *Now Write* on page 75. Have them check to see if their transitions are clear and if they are varied. Ask students to revise their paragraphs if necessary.

2. Stage an event in your classroom that your students can report in the form of a narrative paragraph. For example, have a fellow teacher or a student from another class enter your classroom, shake

hands with you, write on the chalkboard, and remove your chair from the room. Afterward, ask your students to write one paragraph telling what happened by using specific details and effective transitions. Have volunteers read their paragraphs aloud. Comment on good details and transitions.

The Descriptive Paragraph   Pages 79–85

Objectives

1. To use sensory details to create a mood in a descriptive paragraph
2. To use spatial order when organizing descriptive paragraphs
3. To use transitions to indicate spatial order in descriptive paragraphs

Preparing the Students

Ask your class to tell you what they know about descriptive paragraphs. Then read the following selection aloud.

> He opened his eyes again many hours later because he was cold. His head ached and he shivered. The lamp still burned, but its light seemed to have paled. He looked around the room and saw that a hesitant daylight was filtering through the curtains. The room, with the window shut and the lamp burning, was very stuffy. He crawled out of the chair, yawning, and went on unsteady legs to the window. Pulling back the curtains he flung it open. The day had come. A white, shadowless light showed an empty street, blank windows, and shut doors.—JOAN PHIPSON

Ask students how this person must have felt. Also ask them how they felt as they heard the passage. Ask what details account for these feelings. Tell your students that descriptions such as this one by Joan Phipson, arouse images and feelings. Note that Section 8 will show them how to write good descriptive paragraphs.

Part 1

Sensory Perception How To Use Your Senses
in Description

Objective To use sensory details to create a mood in a descriptive
paragraph

Presenting the Lesson 1. Before you read aloud, *Here's the Idea*,
review the vocabulary of the senses on pages 14–17. Explain that sensory details describe specific sights, sounds, textures, tastes, and smells.
Encourage students to be aware of all their senses when they experience something. Ask how sensory details can create a mood.
   2. Read aloud *Check It Out*. Then pair off students to list the
sensory details and write which senses each detail appeals to. As a
class, discuss the mood of each paragraph. Ask which specific words
and details create the mood.
   3. Assign and discuss *Try Your Skill*. You might allow students
to describe a different place. Have volunteers read their lists of details.
   4. Assign *Now Write*. After reading aloud the instructions, suggest
that students select a place where they work, where they babysit,
or where they live. Remind students to follow the steps in *The
Process of Writing*.

Extending the Lesson 1. Compile and duplicate the paragraphs
written in *Now Write* for a class booklet. If you have more than one
class working on this assignment, have them share class booklets so
that students can see a variety of sensory details used in writing.
   2. Have students write a paragraph for a potato chip advertise-
ment. First, give each student a potato chip and tell the class to list
twenty sensory details that describe it. Then tell students to revise
their lists, using only details and words that create a positive, appealing mood. Encourage them to use a dictionary or thesaurus to
choose vivid words. Finally, instruct students to combine the sensory
details with a topic sentence and an ending sentence and write a
descriptive paragraph.

Part 2 **Patterns** How To Use Spatial Order in Description
pp. 82–83

Objective To use spatial order when organizing descriptive paragraphs

Presenting the Lesson 1. Review chronological order as one way to organize writing. Read aloud and discuss *Here's the Idea*. Emphasize the definition of *spatial order*.

2. Read aloud and discuss *Check It Out*. As you read the paragraphs, you might have a student diagram the scene on the chalkboard. In addition to pointing out the spatial order in the paragraph, have your students identify the sensory details.

3. Assign groups of three to work on *Try Your Skill*. Let them discuss a suitable order and complete the exercise. All groups can then share their methods of organization. You might use the chalkboard to diagram a few of the methods.

4. Assign *Now Write*.

Extending the Lesson Hand each student a rock or a sea shell. Tell students to become so thoroughly familiar with their object that they will be able to recognize it later. Have students describe their objects in paragraphs organized by spatial order. Then place all the objects on your desk and ask students to exchange paragraphs. See if students can match the objects with the paragraphs.

Part 3 **Put It There!** How To Use Transitions in Description
pp. 84–85

Objective To use transitions to indicate spatial order in descriptive paragraphs

Presenting the Lesson 1. Read aloud and discuss *Here's the Idea*. Have students write the list of transitions shown on page 84 and keep it in their folders. Ask them to label the list "Transitions in Description." Students will be using this list all year. Ask your students to point out the transitions in the descriptive paragraph.

2. Read aloud and discuss *Check It Out*. Ask the class to identify the transitions used in the paragraph to show spatial relationships.

3. Assign and discuss *Try Your Skill*. Have the class review the list of transitions on page 84. After the students complete the assignment, ask them to read their paragraphs to the class.

4. Assign *Now Write*. Encourage the class to use a variety of transitions. Also refer to *The Process of Writing* covered in Section 6.

Extending the Lesson 1. Have each student write a paragraph describing the photograph on page 128, 152, 174, or 184 of the textbook. Emphasize the need for transitions that show spatial order.

Tell the class to refer to the list on page 84. The paragraphs should have transitions, sensory details, and a definite mood.

2. Draw a pattern using geometric shapes. Allow only one student to look at the drawing, and have that student describe it for the class. As the student describes it, have the class try to duplicate the drawing on their own papers. Afterward, let students compare drawings. Discuss how transitions helped to show them the spatial order of the pattern.

The Explanatory Paragraph   Pages 87–99

Objectives

1. To use clear, logical order in an explanatory *how* paragraph
2. To use transitions that show step-by-step order
3. To understand that the purpose of an explanatory *why* paragraph is to express and explain an opinion
4. To use order of importance for arranging facts and reasons in an explanatory *why* paragraph
5. To use transitions in a *why* paragraph to show reasons and their order of importance
6. To sum up explanatory *why* paragraphs with effective concluding sentences
7. To understand that an explanatory *what* paragraph defines something
8. To write definitions that include both the general class and the specific characteristics of the subject
9. To develop the topic sentence of an explanatory *what* paragraph with supporting facts and figures or personal details

Preparing the Students

Give the class the following problem to solve:

> You have a younger brother who is five years old. His kindergarten teacher told him that he must learn to tie his shoelaces. How would you teach him this simple task?

Have students work in pairs with one student assuming the role of the younger brother and the other student the role of the older sibling. Have the groups act out this teaching/learning experience. They probably will find that it is not easy to explain this task.

Afterward, tell them that the older siblings' words were explanatory. Ask what directions seemed to work best for explanations. Announce that in Section 9 students will learn how to write an explanatory paragraph.

Part 1 **Do It Yourself** How To Plan an Explanation pp. 88–89

Objective To use clear, logical order in an explanatory *how* paragraph

Presenting the Lesson 1. Read aloud and discuss *Here's the Idea.* You may first want to review pages 40–41. Explain that this lesson will deal with only the *how* paragraph and that paragraphs that explain *why* and *what* will be covered later in Section 9. Point out that teaching a small child how to tie his or her shoelaces would be a topic for an explanatory *how* paragraph.

2. After reading the paragraph in *Check It Out,* discuss the logical, sequential order that it follows. Explain that the steps could not be placed in any other order. Ask students if they used a step-by-step order in the shoelace exercise.

3. Read the directions for *Try Your Skill.* (For answers, see Key.) Have students complete this exercise on their own. Then have a volunteer read the steps in logical sequence. Ask the class if the steps are clear.

4. Assign and discuss *Now Write.* After students complete their paragraphs, ask them to read them to classmates seated nearby to see if the listeners can follow the paragraphs easily.

Extending the Lesson 1. Assign demonstration speeches. Students should think of simple tasks they can show the class. These are possible topics: how to wrap a gift, how to build a fire, how to throw a softball, how to tie a knot, how to care for goldfish. Before the speeches, have students first write an explanatory paragraph telling how to perform the task. They should be allowed to refer to their paragraphs when they speak.

2. During your study of Section 9, have students create a bulletin board display on the three kinds of explanatory paragraphs: *how,*

why, and *what.* Have students collect paragraphs of each type for the display. Remind them of these sources: recipes, game directions, and certain magazine articles for *how* paragraphs; editorials, letters to the editor, and campaign literature for *why* paragraphs; and labels, advertisements, brochures, and catalogs for *what* paragraphs. Periodically look over and discuss the posted examples.

Part 2 **Follow Through** How To Use Step-by-Step Order
pp. 90–91

Objective To use transitions that show step-by-step order in an explanation

Presenting the Lesson 1. Read aloud *Here's the Idea,* and review the kinds of transitions the students have learned. Have students copy the list of transitions, label it "Explanatory *How* Transitions," and put it into their folders. Ask the class to revise the second example on page 90 using different transitions for the final sentence.

2. Read and discuss *Check It Out.*

3. Assign and discuss *Try Your Skill.* Collect the papers and read some aloud, pointing out the various transitions that can be used.

4. Assign *Now Write.* Refer students to page 88 for topic ideas. Stress the use of logical, varied transitions.

Extending the Lesson 1. Have students write paragraphs explaining how to make paper airplanes or paper hats. Remind them to include transitions that show step-by-step order. Ask volunteers to read their paragraphs as the rest of the class follows their instructions. Discuss how logical and complete the explanations are.

2. Have groups of three students put these steps in order and add transitions to show step-by-step order.

    a. Water and weed the garden.

    b. Enjoy the taste of home-grown vegetables.

    c. Choose a sunny spot for a vegetable garden.

    d. Sow seeds in rows.

    e. Pick vegetables.

    f. Prepare the ground by turning the soil and raking it.

Part 3 **What Do You Think?** How To State an Opinion
pp. 92–93

Objectives 1. To understand that the purpose of an explanatory *why* paragraph is to express and explain an opinion

2. To use order of importance for arranging facts and reasons in an explanatory *why* paragraph

Presenting the Lesson 1. Before you read aloud *Here's the Idea,* ask if your students have opinions about any of these topics: public transportation, the environment, the price of movie tickets and professional ballgame tickets, or the quality of television programs. Tell them that opinions on these subjects could be presented in explanatory paragraphs. Read *Here's the Idea.* On the chalkboard, write and define *order of importance.* If students have difficulty understanding why the most important point should be at the end of the paragraph, ask them what a reader is most likely to remember after reading a paragraph.

2. Read and discuss *Check It Out.* On the board, write the topic sentence of the paragraph and the reasons used to support the opinion.

3. Assign and discuss *Try Your Skill.*

4. Assign *Now Write.* You might wish to open the topic to include the school.

Extending the Lesson Tell your students that you will present them with an imaginary situation to which they will have to respond. Tell them that you have just spoken to the principal and that he or she reported that all extracurricular sports and activities will be cancelled this year because of lack of funds. Ask students to write one-paragraph letters to the principal stating reasons why the school's extracurricular program should or should not be cancelled. Remind them to write strong topic sentences and to use transitions for presenting their reasons in order of importance.

Part 4 **Speak Out** How To Develop an Opinion pp. 94–95

Objectives 1. To use transitions in a *why* paragraph to show reasons and their order of importance

2. To sum up explanatory *why* paragraphs with effective concluding sentences

Presenting the Lesson 1. Read aloud *Here's the Idea.* Review the kinds of transitions the class has already studied. Ask students to write the new list of transitions, labelled "Explanatory *Why* Transitions," and to keep it in their folders. Point out the two types of transitions.

Refer to page 50 to review the characteristics of a good concluding sentence in a paragraph. Mention that a concluding sentence may restate the topic sentence.

2. Read and discuss *Check It Out*. List the topic sentence, the reasons, and the transitions on the chalkboard.

3. Assign *Try Your Skill*. Emphasize the need for a strong topic sentence, logically ordered reasons, and a good ending sentence. Have students exchange papers and make suggestions for improvement.

4. Assign *Now Write*. You might make a list of current controversial topics on the chalkboard. Before students begin listing reasons, check their topic sentences. The paragraphs may be shared and discussed.

Extending the Lesson Assign a one-paragraph letter-to-the-editor. Before students begin writing, stimulate discussion of town- or school-related issues, such as coed sports teams, the use of city parks, supporting school activities, or keeping the city clean. Then instruct them to write a statement of opinion and to find supporting facts and reasons. Remind them to use transitions and a concluding sentence in their paragraphs. Have students submit these letters to the school or local newspaper and watch for them in print.

Part 5 **On Your Terms** How To State a Definition pp. 96–97

Objectives 1. To understand that an explanatory *what* paragraph defines something

2. To write definitions that include both the general class and the specific characteristics of the subject

Presenting the Lesson 1. Review *how* and *why* explanatory paragraphs and then read aloud *Here's the Idea*. Have the class pay special attention to the three parts of a good definition.

2. Read aloud and discuss *Check It Out*.

3. Assign *Try Your Skill*.

4. Assign *Now Write*. You might suggest that students select an object in the classroom to define.

Extending the Lesson 1. Give each student one volume of an encyclopedia. Have students examine the definitions given in the first paragraph of most articles. Then ask each student to find an interesting entry and to list the word defined in the entry, along with its general class and its specific characteristics. Have students exchange papers and write explanatory *what* paragraphs based on the notes.

2. Hand out slips of paper to each student and ask them to write down the names of three things that might be found in either a workshop or a gym. Collect these slips of paper and put them into a bag. Then have each student draw a piece of paper and write a definition for one of the words on it. Without disclosing the objects, read aloud some of the definitions for the class to identify.

Part 6 **Be Definite** How To Develop a Definition   pp. 98–99

Objective To develop the topic sentence of an explanatory *what* paragraph with supporting facts and figures or personal details

Presenting the Lesson 1. Read aloud and discuss *Here's the Idea*.
2. Read and discuss *Check It Out*.
3. Assign *Try Your Skill*. Discuss examples of details that could be used to develop the definitions.
4. Assign *Now Write*.

Extending the Lesson Write these memorable definitions on the chalkboard.

a) Friendship is a sheltering tree.—SAMUEL COLERIDGE
b) Hope is itself a species of happiness.—SAMUEL JOHNSON

Ask students to develop one of the definitions into a paragraph by adding personal details.

WRITING SECTION 10

What Is a Composition?   Pages 101–107

Objectives

1. To understand the definition of a composition
2. To recognize the three parts of a composition: the introduction, the body, and the conclusion
3. To recognize the three kinds of compositions: narrative, descriptive, and explanatory

Preparing the Students

Draw the following diagram on the chalkboard.

word —→ sentence —→ paragraph —→ COMPOSITION

Explain that just as words make up sentences and sentences make up paragraphs, paragraphs make up compositions. Review what the students have learned about paragraphs, including these terms: topic sentence, concluding sentence, facts, examples, details, and transitions. Tell students that they are now ready to begin writing compositions.

Part 1 **More Ideas at Work** Defining a Composition
pp. 102–103

Objective To understand the definition of a composition

Presenting the Lesson 1. Read aloud *Here's the Idea*. Write the definition of *composition* on the board.

2. Read the composition in *Check It Out*. Note that this composition uses dialogue, which will be discussed later in the textbook. Have students point out the main idea of the composition, as well as the transitions that unify it. Ask how the title helps to convey the main idea of the composition.

3. Assign *Try Your Skill* to be completed by groups of three. See if all groups agree on the answers. If not, have them support their choices.

4. Assign *Now Write*. To stimulate ideas, write headings such as these on the chalkboard:

a humorous experience	a controversial issue
a frightening experience	a difficult problem
a sad experience	a fantastic idea
an interesting place	a complex process

Remind students that their topics must be broad enough for a composition.

Extending the Lesson Check out magazines from your high school library so that each student can look over two magazines during class. Include news magazines, such as *Time* and *Newsweek*; sports magazines, such as *Hot Rod*, *Bike World*, and *Skin Diver*; and fashion magazines, such as *Glamour* and *Seventeen*. Have all students scan these magazines and decide on five interesting ideas for compositions suggested by the magazines. Then pass a ditto master around the class for each student to write his or her topics on. The next day, distribute the dittos and discuss the appropriateness of each topic. Most likely, students will end up with a list of appealing ideas to keep in their folders.

Part 2 **Three-Part Harmony** The Parts of a Composition
pp. 104–105

Objective To recognize the three parts of a composition: the introduction, the body, and the conclusion

Presenting the Lesson 1. Read aloud and discuss *Here's the Idea*. List and define *introduction, body,* and *conclusion* on the chalkboard.

2. Read aloud and discuss the composition in *Check It Out*. Point out that the introduction is the entire first paragraph, not just one sentence. Look again at the introduction, body, and conclusion of the composition on pages 102–103.

3. Discuss the conclusion in *Try Your Skill*. You might have the class suggest an introduction and body to lead up to this last paragraph.

4. Assign *Now Write*.

Extending the Lesson 1. Ask students to clip out short articles from the features section of a newspaper or from *Reader's Digest* or *TV Guide*. Have each student select an article and label its introduction, body, and conclusion. Have students exchange articles with several classmates to check the labels.

2. Duplicate and distribute a well written student composition with its paragraphs jumbled. Have students number the paragraphs in logical order and label the introduction, the paragraphs belonging to the body, and the conclusion. Discuss the effectiveness of each of the three parts.

Part 3 **More Nameplates** Recognizing Three Kinds
of Compositions   pp. 106–107

Objective To recognize the three kinds of compositions: narrative, descriptive, and explanatory.

Presenting the Lesson 1. Read aloud *Here's the Idea*. Review the three kinds of writing on page 40, if necessary.

2. Read aloud and discuss *Check It Out*. In addition, have students identify the introduction, the body, and the conclusion in this explanatory composition.

3. Assign and discuss *Try Your Skill*.

4. Assign *Now Write*. Encourage students to make their notes specific.

Extending the Lesson Have students form groups of three. Visit the library so that each group can search for an example of each of the three kinds of compositions in magazines, newspapers, and books. Have each group list the three composition titles along with a brief summary of each composition. The next day in class, have the groups read the titles of their three kinds of compositions. Let the class guess which kind of composition each title belongs to.

The Narrative Composition Pages 109–119

Objectives

1. To know how to make notes when planning both real and imaginary narratives

2. To select an appropriate point of view for a narrative

3. To write an effective introduction and develop a conflict in the body of a narrative composition

4. To use appropriate transitions in narrative compositions

5. To use dialogue to reveal character

6. To punctuate dialogue properly

7. To understand how to write flashbacks in narrative compositions

8. To write a strong conclusion and an interesting title for a narrative composition

Preparing the Students

Reread the narrative composition entitled "An Unusual Trip" on page 102. On the chalkboard, write the following qualities of a narrative composition learned thus far and discuss them:

A composition is a group of paragraphs dealing with one main subject.

A composition includes an introduction, a body, and a conclusion.

A narrative composition is one of three kinds of compositions.

A narrative composition tells a real or imaginary story in chronological order.

Tell your students that Writing Section 11 will show them more specifically how to plan and write narrative compositions.

Part 1 **Think It Through** How To Plan a Narrative Composition
pp. 110–111

Objective To know how to make notes when planning both real and imaginary narratives

Presenting the Lesson 1. Read aloud and discuss *Here's The Idea.* Write on the board the two ways of making notes for narratives:

for true account details—recall people, places, and events
for story details—invent characters, setting, and plot

2. Read aloud and discuss *Check It Out.*

3. Assign and discuss *Try Your Skill.* Have students write at the top of their papers whether the notes are for a true account or for a story. Ask volunteers to read their notes aloud.

4. Ask students to brainstorm in order to find suitable topics for *Now Write.* Have students use headings (*topic, introduction, body,* and *conclusion*) for their notes.

Extending the Lesson Write a list of ten current television shows on the chalkboard. Assign each student a television show to watch during the week. While viewing the shows, students should make notes on the story details. Have students label the details that would appear in the introduction, the body, and the conclusion of a narrative composition. Ask several students to read the notes they have organized to the class. Discuss how effective these stories would be for narrative compositions.

Objectives 1. To select an appropriate point of view for a narrative composition
2. To write an effective introduction and develop a conflict in the body of a narrative composition
3. To use appropriate transitions in narrative compositions

Presenting the Lesson 1. Read aloud *Here's the Idea*. Review first-person, third-person, and omniscient points of view, and ask when each is appropriate. Discuss the purpose of the introduction and the body in a narrative. Discuss the three kinds of conflict, and ask for examples of each. Refer to the narrative transitions listed on page 76.
2. Read aloud and discuss the paragraph in *Check It Out*.
3. Assign and discuss *Try Your Skill*. Point out that the students must add transitions and details to the paragraph. Discuss why either first-person or omniscient point of view would be most effective here. Collect the narratives and read some aloud to show different ways of developing the idea.
4. Assign *Now Write*. Have students refer to the narrative transitions on page 76.

Extending the Lesson Divide the class into groups of three, and give each group the same short story anthology. Ask the groups to determine the point of view of several short stories by reading the introductions. Also ask students to notice the transitions used in one story. Then have groups compare and defend their conclusions.

Objectives 1. To know how to use dialogue to reveal character
2. To punctuate dialogue properly

Presenting the Lesson 1. Ask pairs of students to write a fictitious situation involving a conflict between two people, such as a son asking his father for the car keys. Then have students act out these conflicts for the other students. Ask what the dialogues reveal about each character.
2. Read aloud *Here's the Idea* and discuss the definition of *dialogue*. Point out that the improvisations that students just performed used dialogue in order to develop the story.

Emphasize the difference between direct quotations and indirect quotations by writing these sentences on the chalkboard:

Eric said, "I'm going home." (direct quotation)
Eric said that he's going home. (indirect quotation)

3. Read aloud *Check It Out*. Refer to the seven basic rules and how they are applied in the dialogue. For another example of dialogue, have students turn to page 103.
4. Assign and discuss *Try Your Skill*. Encourage students to show personality traits through dialogue. Have volunteers read their dialogues aloud.
5. Assign *Now Write*.

Extending the Lesson Hand out Sunday comics to your class. After students have read and examined a comic strip, ask them to write one sentence summarizing the story and one sentence describing each character. Then have students write the dialogue in the form of direct quotations, using proper punctuation. Have them limit their dialogues to one page.

Part 4 **Behind the Times** How To Use a Flashback in a Narrative
pp. 116–117

Objective To understand how to write flashbacks in narrative compositions

Presenting the Lesson 1. Read aloud *Here's the Idea*. Write *flashback* and its definition on the chalkboard. Ask students if they can recall any movies, television shows, or books that use flashbacks. Charles Dickens's *A Christmas Carol* is one famous example. Emphasize the importance of using transitions to identify flashbacks.
2. Read aloud and discuss *Check It Out*. Ask students to point out transitions.
3. Assign *Try Your Skill*. Ask volunteers to read their flashbacks to the class, and have the class comment on the appropriateness of each.
4. Assign *Now Write*.

Extending the Lesson 1. Have students write flashbacks to insert into the narrative "An Unusual Trip" on pages 103–104. Ask students to read their flashbacks to the class.

2. Write the following conflicts on the chalkboard:

   a) Christmas is approaching and a young boy without much money tries to think of a way to give gifts to his family.

   b) An immigrant tries to get all of his family to America.

   c) A pilot tries to land her plane during a heavy storm.

   d) A student feels lonely when she transfers to a new school.

Discuss what flashbacks would be effective for developing each of these conflicts in a narrative.

Part 5 **The Wrap-Up** How To Complete a Narrative Composition pp. 118–119

Objective To write a strong conclusion and an interesting title for a narrative composition

Presenting the Lesson 1. Read aloud and discuss *Here's the Idea.* Emphasize the purpose of the conclusion and the need for consistency.

2. Have students read over the introduction and body of the narrative composition on pages 112–117 before reading the conclusion in *Check It Out.* Discuss the effectiveness of the conclusion and title. You might ask the students to suggest other titles for this story.

3. Assign and discuss *Try Your Skill.* Stress that the conflict should be resolved in an interesting way. Ask volunteers to share their conclusions and titles.

4. Assign *Now Write.* Have students refer to a dictionary or thesaurus for correct spelling and vivid, expressive words.

Extending the Lesson 1. Read aloud several short short stories. Discuss how the conflict is resolved in the conclusion of each story. Ask which stories have surprise endings and which conclusions are most consistent with the rest of the story. Have students suggest alternate titles for the stories.

2. Divide the class into groups and ask the students to read their narratives completed in *Now Write* to each other. Have group members suggest several good titles for each composition. Ask each group to vote on a favorite composition. You might post these favorites on the bulletin board or submit them, with the authors' permission, to the school literary magazine.

The Descriptive Composition
Pages 121–127

Objectives

1. To choose appropriate topics for descriptive compositions
2. To make notes when planning descriptive compositions
3. To learn to write effective introductions for descriptive compositions
4. To use sensory details in the body of a description
5. To organize descriptions in logical order
6. To write a strong conclusion and an interesting title for a descriptive composition

Preparing the Students

Ask students to think of the kind of pizza they like best. Have them describe it, from the kind of crust to the kind of topping. Ask them to use sensory details.

Point out that the process of description that they have used to tell about pizza could also be used when writing compositions. Review the definition of a descriptive composition, and ask how it differs from a narrative composition. Tell students that Writing Section 12 will show them how to write descriptive compositions.

Part 1 **In the Picture** How To Plan a Descriptive Composition
pp. 122–123

Objectives 1. To choose appropriate topics for descriptive compositions
2. To make notes when planning a descriptive composition

Presenting the Lesson 1. Read aloud *Here's the Idea*. Reread the descriptive composition on pages 104–105. Point out that for descriptive compositions the topic must be broad enough. Explain the purpose of the introduction, body, and conclusion in a descriptive composition.

2. Read and discuss the pre-writing notes in *Check It Out*. Point

out the spatial organization in the notes for the body. Have students identify the senses that each detail appeals to.

3. Assign and discuss *Try Your Skill*. List the five senses (sight, hearing, touch, taste, and smell) on the chalkboard to assist students. After they have made their notes, have students decide on the best way to organize them for descriptive compositions.

4. Assign *Now Write*. Write this process on the chalkboard for students to follow.

> Select a topic.
> Narrow the topic.
> List headings on left side of paper.
> List sensory words and details in spatial order.
> Plan the introduction, the body, and the conclusion.

Extending the Lesson   Have students pretend they are preparing a sightseeing brochure for your town. Let groups of two or three choose a local attraction to describe. Ask them to write and organize notes for a descriptive brochure.

Part 2   **Come to Your Senses**   How To Use Sensory Details
pp. 124–125

Objectives   1. To write effective introductions for descriptive compositions
2. To use sensory details when developing the body of a description

Presenting the Lesson   1. Read aloud *Here's the Idea*. Remind students that the introduction should be interesting and should include the topic sentence. Emphasize the need for concrete sensory details in the body of the composition. Refer to the lists of sensory words on pages 16 and 17.

2. Read and discuss *Check It Out*. On the chalkboard, make five columns for the five senses, and have students list the sensory details used in this paragraph in the proper columns.

3. Write the name of your high school on the chalkboard. Ask students to think of one mood, such as excitement or pressure, that would describe the high school. Then have the students brainstorm for sensory details describing the high school. Write these details on the board. Assign *Try Your Skill* to be completed individually.

4. Assign *Now Write*. Write the names of the five senses on the chalkboard, and let students use a thesaurus or dictionary to find and list sensory words.

Extending the Lesson   1. Ask students to write a topic sentence that would summarize a description of their favorite room. Then have them list twenty sensory details to describe the rooms. Encourage them to use vivid words and details that appeal to all senses. Have volunteers read their papers aloud.

2. Divide the class into groups of five and let the groups choose one of these scenes to describe:

> a beach   a football game   a kitchen

Have each group work out an introduction for a descriptive composition. Then assign each member of the group a different sense, and ask him or her to create three sensory details appealing to that sense. Ask the groups to read aloud their fifteen sensory details, as well as their introductions.

Part 3   **A Place in Space**   How To Organize a Description
pp. 126–127

Objectives   1. To organize descriptions in logical order
2. To write a strong conclusion and an interesting title for a descriptive composition

Presenting the Lesson   1. Read aloud *Here's the Idea.* Point out the use of spatial order on pages 124–125 for describing the library. Note that in a well organzed composition, each paragraph focuses on one aspect of the scene. Stress the importance of writing a strong conclusion that summarizes the main idea.

2. Read and discuss *Check It Out.* On the board, write the transitions from the body on pages 124–125 and from the conclusion. Ask students to suggest another title for the description.

3. Assign *Try Your Skill.* Then have students form groups of three and read their paragraphs to each other. Listeners should identify the spatial pattern that is used, as well as the specific transitions that are included in each paragraph.

4. Assign *Now Write.* Write the following key phrases on the chalkboard.

> interesting introduction?
> logical spatial order?
> clear transitions?
> strong conclusion? (Does it summarize your main idea?
>   Does it include your feelings about the subject?)
> suitable title?

Ask students to revise their compositions and exchange them with students seated near them. Have the readers underline words and phrases that are vague or unclear. The compositions should then be returned to the writers for more revision.

Extending the Lesson 1. Have groups of three students write sensory details describing the photographs on pages 108 and 120. Ask them to arrange the details in spatial order.

2. Duplicate and distribute a travel brochure, deleting the conclusion of the description. Have your students write conclusions and titles for the brochures. Then have students share their writings.

The Explanatory Composition
Pages 129–135

Telling *How*

Objectives

1. To know how to plan an explanatory *how* composition
2. To use step-by-step order in writing a *how* composition
3. To use appropriate transitions within and between the paragraphs of a *how* composition

Preparing the Students

Ask the class to pretend that they are teaching young children cursive writing. Ask each student to select a different capital letter of the alphabet and to write that letter on the chalkboard, explaining how it is written. After all the letters have been written, ask what methods students used to tell how to write the letters. Ask if children could have followed the explanations without seeing the letters written. Ask if the explanations were complete and clear.

Then review the definition of the *how* paragraph. Explain that Writing Section 13 will teach students to write an explanatory *how* composition.

Objective To know how to plan an explanatory *how* composition

Presenting the Lesson 1. Read aloud and discuss *Here's the Idea.* Stress the importance of selecting topics that students know well and organizing their notes in step-by-step order.

2. Read aloud and discuss the pre-writing notes in *Check It Out.* Ask how the notes are organized.

3. Assign and discuss *Try Your Skill.* Point out that students must narrow the topics when they write titles. Have students exchange papers with a partner and comment on the following points.

> Is the title clear?
> Are the steps in the proper order?
> Do the notes include necessary materials, tools, or
>   ingredients?
> Are the notes complete?

Notes may then be corrected or revised.

4. Assign *Now Write.* Have students brainstorm for four processes. Remind students that they should choose processes that they know well.

Extending the Lesson Demonstrate one or more processes for your class, such as the following: doing a magic trick, adjusting bicycle brakes, preparing a salad, playing the recorder, making a woodprint. As you demonstrate, have students take notes. Afterward, instruct them to expand, organize, and title their notes, making sure that they are clear and specific. Have students exchange notes to check for clarity.

Part 2 **Step on It!** How To Use Step-by-Step Order
pp. 132–133

Objective To use step-by-step order in writing a *how* composition

Presenting the Lesson 1. Read aloud *Here's the Idea.* Emphasize that the introduction should contain the topic sentence and that each body paragraph should explain a major step.

2. Read and discuss the body paragraphs in *Check It Out.* Point out that because there are three basic steps in the notes on pages 130–131, there are three paragraphs in the body of the composition.

3. Assign and discuss *Try Your Skill*. You might have students form groups of three to organize the notes. Ask the groups to add details and a title. Have volunteers read each group's work aloud.

4. Assign *Now Write*. Remind the students not to write a conclusion yet. Have students exchange papers and comment on the clarity of the explanation.

Extending the Lesson Distribute copies of the text of a repair manual, a cooking lesson, a crafts manual, or a *Mechanix Illustrated* how-to article. Ask students to underline the topic sentence and label the introduction and conclusion. Have them number the steps in the explanation. Write these on the chalkboard. Ask students to evaluate orally the title and the conclusion.

Part 3 **Good Connections** How To Use Transitions
pp. 134–135

Objective To use appropriate transitions within and between the paragraphs of a *how* composition

Presenting the Lesson 1. Read aloud *Here's the Idea*. Have students look over the step-by-step order transitions on page 90. Tell students that they have already used transitions within paragraphs, but transitions are also used to link paragraphs together.

2. Read the instructions in *Check It Out*. Then read the introduction, the body (on pages 132–133), and the conclusion to the class. After students answer the two questions at the end of the conclusion, have them look for transitions in the entire composition.

Also have students notice the interesting, clear writing of the introduction and the strong conclusion. Ask them to identify the topic sentence.

3. Assign and discuss *Try Your Skill*. Suggest that students refer to the transitions on page 90. Stress the need for a variety of transitions in a paragraph. Ask students to compare their paragraphs with those of other students.

4. Assign *Now Write*.

Extending the Lesson Distribute magazines to your students and have them look for how-to articles. Remind them that some *how* explanations may be somewhat abstract, as in "How To Make Friends" or "How To Enjoy Your Summer." Once each student finds an appropriate article, have him or her list the transitions used in it.

The Explanatory Composition
Pages 137–151

Telling *Why*

Objectives

1. To know how to plan a composition that explains an opinion
2. To support an opinion in a *why* composition with reasons, or facts, presented in order of importance
3. To use transitions to indicate order of importance
4. To begin a *why* composition with an effective introduction and end it with a summarizing conclusion

Preparing the Students

Ask for a show of hands on which of the statements below are opinions:

    a. Washington is the capital of the United States. (fact)
    b. Smoking can be harmful to health. (fact)
    c. Current TV programs insult the intelligence. (opinion)
    d. Coke is the best-selling soft drink. (fact)
    e. Many rock lyrics are immoral. (opinion)
    f. The legal drinking age should be raised to 25. (opinion)
    g. Socialized medicine should be adopted in the United States. (opinion)
    h. Shoplifting is on the increase. (fact)

Ask your students to explain the difference between fact and opinion. Emphasize that facts can be proven, but opinions may be debated. Note that statements c, e, f, and g are opinions and that opinions must be supported before others will accept them as true. Tell students that the purpose of an explanatory *why* paragraph is to support an opinion.

Part 1 **In Your View** How To State an Opinion   **pp. 138–139**

Objective To know how to plan a composition that explains an opinion

Presenting the Lesson 1. Read aloud and discuss *Here's the Idea.* Emphasize the importance of stating the opinion clearly in the introduction. Remind students that unless the reader understands the opinion from the very beginning, the supporting material will make little sense.

2. Read and discuss the notes in *Check It Out.* Point out the logical organization of ideas in the body. Discuss the difference between the topic and the introduction.

3. Assign *Try Your Skill.* You may want to assist your students individually with their statements of opinion. Remind them to narrow their topics sufficiently.

4. Assign *Now Write.*

Extending the Lesson 1. Choose a topic for the class to debate. Divide the class into two teams. As your students debate the issue, make notes on the chalkboard of the major arguments used by each side. After the debate, discuss how both sets of notes should be organized for *why* explanations. Ask for suggestions for the introductions and conclusions.

2. Have students form groups of four to debate the opinions stated in their pre-writing notes for *Now Write.* Such discussion and feedback on their ideas can help students to clarify their opinions and think of more reasons. Afterward, they may revise their notes.

Part 2 **For the Defense** How To Support an Opinion
pp. 140–141

Objective To support an opinion in a why composition with reasons or facts, presented in order of importance

Presenting the Lesson 1. Read aloud *Here's the Idea.* Remind the students that by using the strongest, most convincing argument last, it will stay fresh in the reader's mind and therefore have more impact. Stress the importance of developing different reasons in separate paragraphs.

2. Read and discuss *Check It Out.* Point out that each of the three main points is developed in one paragraph. Have students notice that these points are supported with ample facts and reasons.

3. Read the instructions for *Try Your Skill.* After students have organized their lists in order of importance, have them exchange lists and share additional ideas.

4. Assign *Now Write.* Students may need to use the school library

in order to find supporting reasons, facts, and statistics for their compositions. Suggest that if their topics are current ones, they may refer to the *Readers' Guide to Periodical Literature*. The vertical file, which contains pamphlets, may also be helpful. Students who have sufficient reasons and facts about their subjects might spend time revising their paragraphs. Encourage them to check for empty, overloaded, or padded sentences.

Extending the Lesson 1. Clip out the "Letters to the Editor" section from the past week's local newspaper. Hand a letter to each student or to groups of students. Ask the students to write answers to these questions, which should be listed on the chalkboard.

What opinion does the letter state?
What reasons does the letter give to support the opinion?
What facts does the letter give to support the opinion?
Does the letter present enough evidence?
Is each important point developed in a separate paragraph?
Are the supporting points organized in order of importance?
How could the letter be organized better?

Have volunteers read their letters and their answers to the class.

2. Give groups of students this assignment: choose a specific product to advertise, and list convincing reasons why consumers should buy it.

Part 3 **Be Persuasive** How To Use Transitions pp. 142–143

Objectives 1. To use transitions to indicate order of importance
2. To begin a *why* composition with an effective introduction and end it with a summarizing conclusion

Presenting the Lesson 1. Read aloud *Here's the Idea*. Have students review the transitions on page 94. Ask them to find the transitions in the body of the composition on pages 140–141. Discuss the purpose of the introduction and conclusion in an explanatory *why* composition.

2. Read and discuss *Check It Out*. Then read aloud the entire composition, including the body, on pages 140–141. Have students evaluate the title.

3. Assign and discuss *Try Your Skill*.

4. Assign *Now Write*. Remind students that the introduction should be interesting and the opinion clearly stated. Encourage students to think of effective titles.

Extending the Lesson 1. Divide the class into groups. Give each group pamphlets from a different charitable or ecological organization, such as the National Society for the Prevention of Cruelty to Animals or the National Wildlife Federation. Ask the groups to analyze these persuasive pamphlets by writing the topic sentence; labeling the introduction, body, and conclusion; underlining the main points; and writing the number of facts or reasons used to support each main point. Ask the groups to discuss the effectiveness of the supporting reasons and facts. Afterward, have each group read its pamphlet and present its conclusions.

2. Ask your students to pretend that they are editors of the school newspaper. Have them think of someone or some people in the school who should be commended, and write the introduction to an editorial supporting that viewpoint. Remind them to lead up to their statement of opinion in the topic sentence.

The Explanatory Composition
Pages 145–151

Telling *What*

Objectives

1. To know how to plan an explanatory *what* composition
2. To state a definition in the introduction of an explanatory *what* composition
3. To develop the body of an explanatory *what* composition with facts and figures or personal details
4. To summarize the main idea of an explanatory *what* composition in the conclusion

Preparing the Students

Write the following chart on the chalkboard:

General Class	Specific
cats	tiger
flowers	_____
fish	_____
bicycles	_____
movie stars	_____
emotions	_____

Ask volunteers to insert specific items for each general class. Then have each student select a specific word listed on the board and write a definition. Ask students to read their brief definitions to the class.

Point out that an explanatory *what* composition is built upon a definition. Tell students that Writing Section 15 will show them how to write explanatory *what* compositions.

Part 1 **What's What?** How To Plan a Definition   pp. 146–147

Objective To know how to plan an explanatory *what* composition

Presenting the Lesson 1. After reading aloud *Here's the Idea*, discuss the importance of definitions. Have students give examples of situations where not knowing a definition causes problems, such as a driver not knowing what a particular traffic sign means, or someone who is cooking not knowing what a certain ingredient is. Stress the importance of finding a topic that is broad enough for a composition. Also point out the purpose of the introduction, body, and conclusion in an explanatory *what* composition.

2. Read and discuss *Check It Out*. Point out the organization of the notes, and explain that each main heading will be developed into a paragraph in the composition.

3. Assign and discuss *Try Your Skill*. Suggest that students refer to dictionaries and encyclopedias for information. This activity might be assigned for homework. Volunteers may read their notes aloud the next day in class.

4. Assign *Now Write*. Have students brainstorm in order to think of suitable topics. First have students list five to ten topics that are related to jobs or hobbies. Then ask students to select only one topic. Have students pair off to discuss each other's notes and try to add more details or facts and figures.

Extending the Lesson 1. Ask students to select the topics below that would be appropriate for explanatory *what* compositions.

prejudice	making sand paintings
happiness	the need for daycare
taking good photos	pet therapy
a TV studio	music as relaxation
a construction site	the school cafeteria
my first day of school	a day I would like to forget

As a review of all types of compositions, have your students identify the type of composition that suits each topic best.

2. Have one student make notes on the chalkboard as the others volunteer all the information they know about superheroes. Afterward, have students look over the notes and suggest how to organize them into the introduction, body, and conclusion of a composition. Ask students to copy these reorganized notes.

Part 2 **For the Record** How To State a Definition pp. 148–149

Objective To state a definition in the introduction of an explanatory *what* composition

Presenting the Lesson 1. Read aloud *Here's the Idea.* Emphasize that the definition serves as the topic sentence for an explanatory *what* composition.

2. Read and discuss *Check It Out.* You might have students look at page 146 for the notes for the introduction.

3. Assign and discuss *Try Your Skill.* Encourage students to use their own words rather than copying a definition from a reference book. Have volunteers read their definitions aloud.

4. Assign *Now Write.* After students complete the activity, have them exchange introductions. Students should check for a clear definition naming the subject, its general class and its particular characteristics.

Extending the Lesson 1. Select a filmstrip or a movie that tells about a country, a literary form, a scientific discovery, or a historical period. Make certain that the subject matter is simple but appealing. Show the film and ask students to make notes for an explanatory *what* composition on the subject. The notes should include details or facts and figures from the film. Finally, students should write definitions and introductions for the composition. You may need to show the film twice so students can pick out enough details.

2. Ask students to "invent" a gadget of the future. Have them write definitions of these gadgets and share them with the rest of the class.

3. Ask students to write an introduction for a composition explaining superheroes. These introductions should be based on the notes compiled in the preceding Extending the Lesson.

Part 3 **Ways and Means** How To Develop a Definition
pp. 150–151

Objectives   1. To develop the body of an explanatory *what* composition with facts and figures or personal details

2. To summarize the main idea of an explanatory *what* composition in the conclusion

Presenting the Lesson   1. Read aloud *Here's the Idea*. Point out the two possible ways to develop a *what* composition. Refer to the paragraph on page 97 as an example of development by facts. Refer to the paragraph on page 98 as an example of development by personal detail.

2. Read and discuss *Check It Out*. Discuss how the definition is developed, and point out how paragraphs are organized around main points.

3. Assign and discuss *Try Your Skill*. Students may refer to dictionaries after they have written their definitions.

4. Assign *Now Write*. First have the students read their notes. They might want to add personal details or facts and figures.

Extending the Lesson   Have students select a personality trait that they wish they did not have, such as stubbornness, laziness, or aggressiveness. Ask them to write a definition of that trait and to summarize three incidents when they exhibited that trait. Finally, have them think of a title for an explanatory *what* composition on the topic. Discuss how these notes could be used to write a composition.

Letters, Applications, and Résumés
Pages 153–173

Objectives

1. To identify and use correctly the five parts of a friendly letter
2. To address envelopes correctly
3. To gain skill in writing correct business letters
4. To know how to write a letter of inquiry to a school
5. To know how to write a letter of inquiry about employment
6. To gain skill in writing job applications
7. To know how to prepare a résumé

Preparing the Students

Ask students to raise their hands if they have ever written notes to friends, written thank-you notes for gifts, written letters asking about schools, or written job applications. Then ask students to raise their hands if they think they will ever need to write one of these kinds of letters.

Point out the importance of writing correct letters. Ask students what kind of impression a well written letter makes on an employer, a gift giver, or a college official. Explain that Writing Section 16 will explain how to prepare letters, applications, and résumés.

Part 1 **A Better Letter** How To Write Friendly Letters
pp. 154–156

Objective To identify and use correctly the five parts of a friendly letter

Presenting the Lesson 1. Read aloud *Here's the idea.* On the chalkboard diagram and label the five main parts of a friendly letter. Have students define these terms. Discuss different types of friendly letters, and ask students to suggest specific situations when each would be appropriate.

2. Read and dicuss the friendly letter in *Check It Out.* Have students notice the placement of the heading, salutation, body, closing,

and signature. Point out that there are no abbreviations in the heading, that the salutation is followed by a comma, that each paragraph is indented, that the first letter of the closing is capitalized, and that only the first name is used for the signature.

3. After students complete *Try Your Skill*, have five volunteers go to the chalkboard. Assign each volunteer one of the five parts of a friendly letter. Have them write their parts on the chalkboard in consecutive order, beginning with the heading. Then have the class compare their letters with the one written on the chalkboard and make any necessary corrections.

4. Assign *Now Write*. Have the students brainstorm for ideas. First, have them think of the names of five out-of-town friends or relatives. Then ask them to select one of the names and think of what they would like to say to this person.

Extending the Lesson 1. Play a game with your class to quiz them on definitions. Have each student write five questions and answers based on the information on pages 154–155. Collect these papers and use them to question two teams for a "Jeopardy" game. Read the answers, and ask the two teams alternately for the proper questions. Keep a running total of the number of correct responses from each team.

2. One week before your school's open house or parent-teacher conferences, assign this exercise. Have students write letters to their parents, inviting them to the school function. List necessary information, such as the date, time, place, and agenda, on the chalkboard. You may also want to write sample body paragraphs on the board. Remind students to position, punctuate, and capitalize each part of the letter correctly.

Part 2   **A Mailing List**   How To Prepare Letters for the Mail
pp. 157–158

Objective   To address envelopes correctly

Presenting the Lesson 1. Read aloud and discuss *Here's the Idea*. Use a piece of typing paper to demonstrate how to fold a letter and insert it into an envelope.

2. Discuss the questions at the end of *Check It Out*. Point out the placement of the two addresses. Note that state names are now abbreviated with two capital letters and no periods. These state abbreviations are listed on page 484 of the textbook.

3. Assign *Try Your Skill*. Have students divide a piece of notebook paper into thirds with two horizontal lines. On the back of the paper, they should do the same. Tell students to pretend that they have six envelopes. After the students unjumble the addresses and write them correctly on their "envelopes," have volunteers write the correct forms for the envelopes on the chalkboard.

4. Assign *Now Write*.

Extending the Lesson   Ask students to take out their letters written for the preceding Extending the Lesson. Give each student an envelope or ask each student to bring an envelope to class. Have students address the envelopes to their parents and use the school address as the return address. If you can obtain permission, have the letters mailed to the parents at the school's expense.

Part 3   **Business Is Business**   How To Write Business Letters
pp. 159–161

Objective   To gain skill in writing correct business letters

Presenting the Lesson   1. Read aloud *Here's the Idea*. Discuss the purpose of a business letter and how a business letter differs from a friendly letter. On the chalkboard, diagram the two forms for a business letter. Ask students to define *inside address* and discuss the differences between a heading and an inside address.

2. Read and discuss the business letter in *Check It Out*. Point out the clear, direct language of the letter.

3. Assign and discuss *Try Your Skill*. Have students identify the purpose of the letter. Point out that the letter contains many errors. Discuss the correct form.

4. Assign *Now Write*. Ask students to list four defective items that they have owned and then to write a letter of complaint to the manufacturer of one of the items. Students may invent names and addresses of manufacturers for this purpose.

Extending the Lesson   1. Ask students to think of a TV program that they find either especially good or especially objectionable. Have them write letters to the network station, requesting either that the show be continued or that it be cancelled. List the addresses of the four network stations on the chalkboard.

2. Have students think of a city or state they would like to visit. Instruct them to write letters to the chamber of commerce or department of tourism for that city or state to ask for travel information.

Objective To know how to write a letter of inquiry to a school

Presenting the Lesson 1. Read aloud and discuss *Here's the Idea.* Point out that ideally a letter to a school should be typed.
2. Read and discuss *Check It Out.* Ask students if the letter follows the four guidelines on the preceding page. Ask the class whether the letter uses the block or the modified block form.
3. Assign and discuss *Try Your Skill.* After students have completed their final draft, ask those who chose the first situation to form a group. Likewise, have students who selected the other two situations to form separate groups. Ask the groups to agree on the correct form for their letter.
4. Assign *Now Write.* You might provide a copy of the *Barron's* or *Lovejoy's* college guide.

Extending the Lesson Encourage your students to send their letters written for *Now Write.* First, have a conference with each student in order to revise if necessary and proofread the inquiry. Students may then write final drafts and mail them.

Part 5 **Help Wanted** How To Write a Letter About Employment
pp. 165–167

Objective To know how to write a letter of inquiry about employment

Presenting the Lesson 1. Read aloud *Here's the Idea.* Stress the importance of accuracy in spelling and mechanics, precision in penmanship, and clarity in sentence structure. Point out that writing this type of business letter is an important first step toward finding a job.
2. Read and discuss *Check It Out.* Ask students if the letter includes all six items listed on page 165. Ask how the information is organized. Point out the clear, direct style of the letter, as well as the block form.
3. Assign *Try Your Skill.* Have students pair off and take turns pretending to be the employer. Have them comment on each other's letters and check for the six items listed on page 165.
4. Assign *Now Write.* Suggest that students first list answers to the questions on page 165. Then students may write their rough drafts and compare them with drafts composed by other students.

After all corrections have been made, students may write their final drafts.

Extending the Lesson If you have a vocational counselor at your school, ask him or her to speak to your class about the first steps in applying for a job. The presentation might explain how many letters to send to different companies, how to keep files of letters sent to companies, and tips for writing successful letters.

Part 6 **Apply Yourself** How To Complete a Job Application
pp. 168–170

Objective To gain skill in writing job applications

Presenting the Lesson 1. Read aloud and discuss *Here's the Idea*.

2. Read and discuss *Check It Out*. Point out that the answers are printed, not written.

3. Before you assign *Try Your Skill*, duplicate the sample application on the last page of this book. (The publisher grants permission to the classroom teacher to reproduce this page.) Have students complete the application. They should refer to the four guidelines listed on pages 168–169. Remind students that the people whom they intend to use as references should be consulted before their names are written on applications. When students finish the exercise, have them exchange applications to proofread and note confusing answers.

4. For the *Now Write* exercise, ask the manager of a local Mc-Donald's or department store for applications. Assign *Now Write*. Pair students to proofread each other's applications.

Extending the Lesson If students are interested in finding jobs in the community, have them write and send letters to potential employers requesting job applications. In preparation for filling out the applications, have students list the information noted on page 168. When students receive their applications, have them fill in their answers. You might check over the applications before students deliver them to the businesses.

Part 7 **Speak for Yourself** How To Write a Résumé
pp. 171–173

Objective To know how to prepare a résumé

Presenting the Lesson 1. Read aloud *Here's the Idea*. Ask students to define *résumé* (a French word meaning "summary") and explain the difference between an application for employment and a résumé. Remind students to ask permission before writing their references' names on the résumé.

2. Read and discuss *Check It Out*. Ask why an employer would find this résumé helpful.

3. Assign *Try Your Skill*. Have your class rewrite the entire résumé, adding the additional information to it. Ask students to exchange papers and to check for proper placement and clear wording.

4. Assign *Now Write*.

Extending the Lesson Have pairs of students take turns playing the role of employer and interviewing each other, using the applications and résumés they wrote. In preparation for the interview, ask students to study their classmates' applications and résumés, and to write a few questions to ask during the interview.

WRITING SECTION 17

Using a Dictionary   Pages 175–183

Objectives

1. To recognize the basic characteristics of a dictionary
2. To understand the information contained in dictionary entries
3. To gain skill in using context to determine the correct definition of a word

Preparing the Students

Bring to class as many different types of dictionaries as you can. For example, ask to borrow the unabridged dictionary from the school library. Try to collect enough dictionaries so that each student can use one. If you cannot find enough, have students share.

Have students turn to the table of contents of the dictionary. Ask volunteers to identify the different sections in their dictionaries. Point out that while some dictionaries have special sections about population, others have sections about geographical names. Note that a few dictionaries have sections on colleges; others have sections on foreign words and phrases.

Point out that while many students think that dictionaries contain only words and definitions, dictionaries actually have far more to offer. Ask students to think of other possible uses for dictionaries. Explain that Writing Section 17 will help students to use dictionaries efficiently.

Part 1 **From A to Z** How To Use a Dictionary pp. 176–177

Objective To recognize the basic characteristics of a dictionary

Presenting the Lesson 1. Read aloud *Here's the Idea*. Show students the difference between an unabridged dictionary and an abridged dictionary. Compare the number of words and pages each contains. Next emphasize the purpose of guide words. Tell students they can save time by looking at the guide words rather than at words elsewhere on the pages.

2. Read and discuss *Check It Out*. Write the special symbols on the board and have students try to identify what each one stands for. If students have dictionaries, have them study the key to abbreviations and labels used in the dictionary.

3. Assign *Try Your Skill*. Have one student read the alphabetized list to the entire class.

4. Assign *Now Write*.

Extending the Lesson 1. List the following guide words on the chalkboard:

pen / pepper   ear / echo   love / loyal
third / three   curtain / cut   siren / skate

Have each student write three words that would appear on the page headed by each set of guide words. Ask students to share their answers.

2. Ask each student to give a sales pitch for buying a dictionary. In preparation, instruct the class to list as many uses for the dictionary as they can think of. Encourage your students to use a clever style by including slogans and catchy introductions in their sales talks.

Objective To understand the information contained in dictionary entries

Presenting the Lesson 1. Point out that the word *entry* means not only the word that students are looking for, but also everything that is written about the word. Read aloud and discuss *Here's the Idea*. You may wish to discuss one concept at a time and refer immediately to the sample entry in *Check It Out*.

Write these terms on the chalkboard: *entry word, pronunciation, part of speech, special forms, origin, definition, synonym,* and *antonym*. Make sure students can define these terms.

2. Read the entry in *Check It Out*. As you read it, whenever you approach a symbol, ask students what it means. Have students answer the questions at the end of this entry.

3. Assign *Try Your Skill*. Have students consult with you if they see symbols that they cannot identify. When students have finished, ask volunteers to read the answers aloud.

4. Distribute dictionaries and assign *Now Write*. You may find that you need to review terms such as *syllable* and *part of speech*.

Extending the Lesson 1. Have groups of four students investigate the origins, pronunciations, parts of speech, and definitions of these words: *extort, corsage, fender, salary, strategy,* and *volcano*. Afterward, ask groups to compare their findings.

2. Allow each student to write four dictionary entries for current slang or colloquial words, such as *jock* or *deejay*. Instruct them to follow dictionary form, including the entry word, pronunciation, imaginary origin, part of speech, and definition. You might compile the best entries into a dictionary of current slang.

Objective To gain skill in using context to determine the correct definition of a word

Presenting the Lesson 1. Ask the class if they have ever had difficulty in finding the right meaning for a word in a certain context. Read *Here's the Idea*. Ask a student to read the first sentence using the word *set*. Discuss the meaning. Follow this procedure with the remaining five sentences. If students have dictionaries, you might ask them to locate other words with many meanings.

Write *homograph* on the chalkboard and explain its definition. If students have dictionaries, have them look up the word *bark* and find the origins of the three homographs. See if students can point out other homographs in the dictionary.

2. Read and discuss *Check It Out*. As you read aloud, review what the symbols mean. You might have students make up sentences for each meaning of *stem*.

3. Assign and discuss *Try Your Skill*. Have students work in pairs. Advise them to decide first on the part of speech of the word *spell* in each sentence. Have students share their answers.

4. Assign *Now Write*.

Extending the Lesson Using the dictionary, have students find two fairly common words that have more than one meaning. Have students write both words on a scrap of paper. Collect these and have each student draw a paper from a bag or shoebox. Then ask students to look up the two words, list two definitions for each word, and write sentences using each meaning. Have students share their definitions and sentences with the rest of the class.

Using the Library

Pages 185–197

Objectives

1. To understand the library system for arranging and shelving fiction and nonfiction books
2. To use the library's card catalog to locate books
3. To understand the organization and content of encyclopedias
4. To know how to use specific types of reference books

Preparing the Students

Ask each student to draw a map of the school library. Students should label the check-out desk, fiction shelves, nonfiction shelves, magazine section, reference area, recording section, and any other parts they know.

After students have completed this assignment, have them compare their maps. See if any two are alike. Ask if your class can tell you where to find the novels, the reference books, the vertical (pamphlet) file, the copier (if there is one), and the card catalog. If the class is familiar with the layout of the library, ask them where specific kinds of books are located.

Ask the student who drew the most accurate map to copy it onto a ditto master. Distribute copies for students to keep. Explain that Writing Section 18 will help students to use their library more efficiently.

Part 1 **Know It All** How To Find What You Need **pp. 186–188**

Objective To understand the library system for arranging fiction and nonfiction books

Presenting the Lesson 1. Before you begin *Here's the Idea*, ask students to define *fiction* and *nonfiction* and give examples. Then read aloud *Here's the Idea*. Emphasize that fiction and nonfiction books are always shelved separately. Discuss the Dewey Decimal System, pointing out the ten categories listed on page 186. After explaining call numbers, have the class look at the model of a book. Show the spine of a real book, and ask students to explain its call number.

2. Discuss the two questions in *Check It Out*. Ask students why the nonfiction books were assigned those Dewey Decimal categories.

3. Assign and discuss *Try Your Skill*. (For answers, see Key.)

4. Assign *Now Write* after your class tours the school library. Then have students add more specific information to their library maps.

Extending the Lesson 1. If you have a public library in your community, contact the library director and ask if your class might visit for an afternoon. Arrange for a brief tour, showing where material is located and how to obtain a library card.

2. At the library, have each student select one book for each Dewey Decimal category and write its title, author, and call number. In class, have students read some of their titles. Ask the rest of the class to guess the Dewey Decimal category.

Objective To use the library's card catalog to locate books

Presenting the Lesson 1. Read aloud *Here's the Idea.* Ask students why three kinds of cards are needed. On the chalkboard, write the three types of cards: author, title, and subject. Below each, diagram the contents of the card. Point out that on the author card, the title is found underneath the author's name, and it is sometimes printed in lower case letters. Also review the purpose of cross reference cards and guide cards.

2. Read and discuss *Check It Out.* First have students identify the book's call number, author, title, publishing company, copyright date, and number of pages. Mention that *ill* means that the book is illustrated, and *24cm* is the height of the book. Point out the placement of all information on each of the three cards.

3. Assign *Try Your Skill.* Suggest that students refer to the three models on page 190. Ask that they create additional details, such as the publishing company, copyright date, and number of pages. You might point out that 651.26 and En35c are both parts of the call number. Have students exchange papers and see if they can identify all three types of cards.

4. Assign *Now Write.* You might assign this exercise as homework so that students will use the career sections of the card catalog at different times.

Extending the Lesson 1. Have groups of two or three students make posters illustrating the kinds of cards in the card catalog. You might allow students to use humorous book titles and authors' names on the posters. Display them in class or in the library.

2. Show sample cards on the opaque projector. Ask the class to identify whether each card is an author, title, or subject card. Also quiz students on other information contained on the card.

3. Have students use the card catalog to find three books that pertain to each of these categories.

books by James Michener   books about radio
books with titles beginning   novels with titles starting
    with the word *Light*   with *Around*
books about Bermuda

Objective To understand the organization and content of encyclopedias

Presenting the Lesson 1. Read aloud *Here's the Idea*. Encourage students to use the World Book Encyclopedia, Collier's Encyclopedia, and Britannica Junior Encyclopaedia, since they will have less difficulty reading these than they will with other encyclopedias in the library. As you read the text you might wish to use the C volume of an encyclopedia. Turn to "Careers" and point out the guide words and the parts of the article.

Discuss the best way to use encyclopedias. Note that students sometimes rely on encyclopedias only, without referring to other books and magazines in the library. Tell students that even though encyclopedias are useful, they often are condensed, and should be used as a starting point. Have students pay special attention to the discussion of plagiarism in the last paragraph of *Here's the Idea*.

2. Take your students to the school library and assign *Check It Out*. Explain that recognizing key words is important when looking for a subject in an encyclopedia.

3. Assign and discuss *Try Your Skill*. (For answers, see Key.) You may want to have students check their answers in the encyclopedia.

4. Assign *Now Write*. This may be an out-of-class assignment unless your class can visit the library.

5. Assign *Write Again*.

Extending the Lesson 1. Give each student a volume of an encyclopedia. Ask students to make up five questions about information in their volume. Collect these questions, as well as all encyclopedias, and distribute the questions to different students. Then have students locate the answers in the encyclopedia. Ask them to list the encyclopedia, the number and guide letter of the volume, the page number, and the entry title they used to answer each question.

2. Use the opaque projector to show your class the entries from three different encyclopedias on a topic such as *bowling*. Ask them to compare and contrast the encyclopedias in the areas of entry length, amount of information, type of information, extent of illustration, and simplicity of style.

Objective To know how to use specific types of reference books

Presenting the Lesson 1. As you read *Here's the Idea,* list on the chalkboard the special types of reference books. You might bring examples of each to class. Ask students if they have ever used these reference works and where the books are located in your school or public library. Discuss how and when to use each type.

2. Have students study the portion of the *Readers' Guide* listed in *Check It Out.* Point out that the title of the article is always printed first, following the boldly printed guide words. The magazine title is always abbreviated. You might borrow a volume of the *Readers' Guide* from your school library to show students the magazine abbreviations listed in the front. Explain that the issue date is always listed last. Write the abbreviations for the months on the chalkboard. Finally, tell students that the page numbers are listed to the right of the colon, and the number to the left of the colon is the volume number.

3. Assign and discuss *Try Your Skill.* (For answers, see Key.)

4. Assign *Now Write.*

Extending the Lesson 1. Have students answer questions 1–6 in *Try Your Skill.* They should list the source of each answer: its title, call number, volume number, and page number.

2. Hold a reference work treasure hunt. Divide the class into groups and have each group write eight questions on these subjects:

> two world events that happened last year
> two famous people
> two places in other countries
> two events in local history

Have groups exchange lists of questions and find the answers in special reference works in the library. Ask groups to list their sources along with their answers. See which group finishes first.

3. Have students use the *Readers' Guide* to find three magazine articles on each of these topics.

> soccer   art
> Australia   plants

Ask students to list the titles of the articles (in quotation marks), the magazines (underlined), the issue dates, and the page numbers.

Writing a Report

Objectives

1. To know how to narrow a subject and find sources for a report
2. To write bibliography cards and note cards correctly
3. To organize note cards by topic
4. To gain skill in writing outlines
5. To write an introduction to a report
6. To gain skill in writing the body of a report from the outline and note cards
7. To write a conclusion for a report
8. To use footnotes correctly in a report
9. To prepare a bibliography for a report

Preparing the Students

Unfortunately, many students think of writing a report as a tiresome, long task that proves they have spent many hours working in the library. Stress that writing a report need not involve endless time in the library. Discuss writing a report as a means of discovery about a particular topic of interest to the student.

In order to motivate the class, hand out thirty to fifty copies of current magazines from the school library. Have each student list ten to twenty topics that they notice as they peruse the magazines. Then spend the class period or several periods discussing some of these topics. Ask students which topics they would like to learn more about. The discussions will help students to find interesting topics and to become familiar with a few topics in depth.

Explain that the class will be writing reports and that Writing Section 19 will teach everything from how to find topics to how to write final drafts. Note that the process described in this section can be used for reports in other classes as well.

Part 1 **A Wise Choice** How To Begin Research for a Report
pp. 200–202

Objective To know how to narrow a subject and find sources for a report

Presenting the Lesson 1. Read aloud *Here's the Idea*. Discuss the difference between a composition and a report. Note that a report is factual and requires library research. Review the Dewey Decimal System and the different reference works students might use to research their topics.

2. Read aloud and discuss *Check It Out*. Have students notice that there are five different kinds of sources listed. Ask where these sources are located in the library.

3. Assign *Try Your Skill*. Have students form groups of three. Ask each group to narrow one subject and list three possible sources. Discuss all six topics with the class after the groups have completed this assignment.

4. Assign *Now Write*. You might ask students to choose topics that appealed to them when they discussed the magazine articles. Have students work in the library during the class period. Make sure that students have narrowed their topics sufficiently.

Extending the Lesson Have each student help a partner by finding three more sources on his or her partner's topic. Students will then have a total of six sources.

Part 2 **In Your Own Words** How To Take Notes for a Report
pp. 203–205

Objective To write bibliography cards and note cards correctly

Presenting the Lesson 1. Read aloud *Here's the Idea*. Ask students what information belongs on bibliography cards. Point out that if students cannot afford or cannot find index cards, they may cut notebook paper into $3'' \times 5''$ pieces. Emphasize that only one source should be placed on a card. Ask students the purpose of note cards. Explain why each card should contain only one idea. Tell students that if they copy material directly from a source onto a card, this material should have quotation marks around it. Explain that even if the material is stated in the student's own words, it still needs the code number from the source. Lead into a discussion of plagiarism. Make sure that students understand that plagiarism is a serious form of cheating. State your school's penalty for plagiarism.

2. Read and discuss *Check It Out*. Have the class check to see if each card follows the rules listed on page 203. Explain that the numbers in the upper right-hand corners are used to identify the sources.

Have students identify the source of the note card on page 205. Mention that the page number should be placed in the lower right-hand corner to avoid confusion with the source number. Ask students the purpose of the heading "origin of fund" on the card.

3. Assign and discuss *Try Your Skill*. Have students draw two rectangles for the bibliography card and the note card. Have the class follow the form of the examples on page 205. Check each student's card, and show accurate ones on the opaque projector.

4. Assign *Now Write*. Accompany students to the library and be available to answer questions.

Extending the Lesson 1. Demonstrate the process of taking notes for a report. Using student examples, write the notes on the chalkboard or make transparencies of bibliography cards and note cards to show on the overhead projector. Explain how the student narrowed a subject, found sources, listed them on bibliography cards, read sources, and took notes.

2. Give students practice in note-taking by duplicating and distributing a brief encyclopedia entry, a brief magazine article, and a biographical reference book entry about the same person. Ask students to take notes and make note cards. Remind them to use their own words whenever possible, to include quotation marks where needed, and to include only one idea on each card. When students have finished, discuss which information belongs on note cards, and have students read sample cards aloud.

Part 3 **Sort It Out** How To Organize Information pp. 206–207

Objective To organize note cards by topic

Presenting the Lesson 1. Read aloud *Here's the Idea*. Note that a few stray cards may not relate to any category. These cards may eventually be placed in one of the piles, or they may be discarded.

2. Read and discuss *Check It Out*. Have students notice how clear the author's main ideas are.

3. Have students form groups of three to complete *Try Your Skill*. Have groups share their sentences and as a class, agree on the best answers.

4. Assign *Now Write*. After students have finished, have them exchange their work. Ask students to check for logical organization. Caution students that if they have more than seven piles of cards,

their papers may become too long. Have them attempt to organize three to seven piles of cards.

Extending the Lesson   1. Hold conferences to evaluate the students' note cards. You might evaluate in two areas: the quality of the note-taking and the organization of the notes.

2. Have students organize the following notes into two separate categories. Ask them to write sentences that summarize each group of notes. The topic of the report is the Olympic Games.

Begun in 1896	Revival of Games of ancient Greeks
More female competitors	Continuing improvement in performance
More sports and events	More athletes from more nations
First Games in Athens	Thirteen nations in first Games
	Nine sports in first Games

Part 4   **The Framework**   How To Make an Outline for a Report
pp. 208–210

Objective   To gain skill in writing outlines

Presenting the Lesson   1. Read aloud and discuss *Here's the Idea*.
2. Have students examine the sample outline in *Check It Out*. Ask students to explain how the outline is organized. Ask if the outline follows all the guidelines explained on page 208. Note that this is a topic outline rather than a sentence outline.
3. Read aloud and assign *Try Your Skill*. You may want to ask the class to give you directions while you write the outline on the chalkboard, or you might have volunteers write their outlines on the board. Discuss the most logical way to write the outline.
4. Assign *Now Write*.

Extending the Lesson   1. After making their outlines, students may notice that they need more facts or examples. Give students one class period in the library to find additional information. Have them add the information to their outlines.
2. Duplicate brief encyclopedia entries and ask students to outline them. Collect the outlines and reproduce especially good ones to discuss as models.

Part 5

First Impressions How To Write an Introduction
pp. 211–213

Objective To write an introduction to a report

Presenting the Lesson 1. Read aloud *Here's the Idea*. Ask students the purpose of the introduction in a report. Stress that students should not use first-person (*I, me, my*) or second-person (*you, your*). Explain that introductions should be exciting and interesting enough to catch the reader's attention.

2. Read and discuss the first two paragraphs of the sample report in *Check It Out*. Have students compare these paragraphs with sections I and II of the outline on page 209. Have students notice the corrections made in this sample rough draft. Ask students which sentence in the introduction best sets forth the topic of the report.

3. Assign and discuss *Try Your Skill*. After students complete this assignment, ask them where they placed the main idea. Have students exchange paragraphs in order to see how others wrote the same information in paragraph form.

4. Assign *Now Write*. Check your students' outlines before they begin their introductions. If necessary, have students revise their outlines.

Extending the Lesson 1. Have students exchange introductory paragraphs. See if the readers can identify the main idea. If they cannot, the writer should revise the introduction so that the main idea is clearly stated.

2. Have students write an introduction to a report on volcanoes. Ask them to use these facts.

    1. The most recent eruption of a volcano was that of Mt. St. Helens in 1980.

    2. There are 850 active volcanoes in the world.

Part 6 **For the Most Part** How To Write the Body and Conclusion
pp. 214–216

Objectives 1. To gain skill in writing the body of a report from the outline and note cards
2. To write a conclusion for a report

Presenting the Lesson 1. Read aloud *Here's The Idea*. Emphasize that one main idea is developed in each paragraph of a report. Note, too, that each paragraph should contain a beginnng, a middle, and an end. Ask students the purpose of the conclusion in a report.

2. Read and discuss the sample first draft in *Check It Out*.

3. Assign *Try Your Skill*. Have students refer to all the *Try Your Skill* exercises in this section. Their conclusions should make general statements about different types of heroes. Ask for volunteers to read their conclusions to the class.

4. Assign *Now Write*. Stress that sentences should be clear and that plagiarism should be avoided. You will probably want to assist your students individually with this assignment. You might schedule conferences to discuss the body and the conclusion of each student's report. The Handbook Section of the textbook will be helpful at this time. You can refer students with specific usage problems to the corresponding handbook sections.

Extending the Lesson 1. Write two sentence fragments on the chalkboard: "What I like most about your report is . . ." and "I want to know more about . . ." Pair students to read each other's rough drafts. Then ask each student to complete these partial statements with constructive comments about the other person's report.

2. Jumble the paragraphs of a student report and show it on the opaque projector or on ditto copies. Ask students to put the paragraphs in the proper order and to evaluate the effectiveness of the conclusion.

3. Read aloud the concluding paragraphs of several chapters in a history textbook. Discuss how effectively each summarizes a main idea.

Part 7 **Credit Lines** How To Finish a Report pp. 217–222

Objectives 1. To use footnotes correctly in a report
2. To prepare a bibliography for a report

Presenting the Lesson 1. Read aloud *Here's the Idea*. It may take more than one reading for the class to understand these concepts. Ask students why footnotes and a bibliography are used in a report. Write more examples of footnotes and bibliography entries on the chalkboard. The textbook gives students a simple way of handling footnotes. If your class is ready for additional instructions, you may want to explain footnoting at the bottom of the page or footnoting ideas as well as quotations.

2. Read and discuss *Check It Out*. Explain how the bibliography entries would be written if they were used as footnotes.

3. Assign *Try Your Skill*. Have one volunteer go to the chalkboard and write the footnote entry. Then have another volunteer write the bibliography entry. Ask if any corrections are needed.

Extending the Lesson 1. Invite students who wrote especially good reports to read them to the class. Just as the class learned about the Carnegie Hero Fund from the textbook, they can also learn about their classmates' topics. A similar exercise is to read a few good reports yourself. After a report is read, ask what the class especially liked about the report.

2. Have groups of students make posters illustrating the forms for footnotes and bibliographies. Allow the class to use humorous titles and authors' names. Display the posters in the classroom.

The Sentence and Its Parts
Pages 235–258

Objectives

1. To distinguish between fragments and complete sentences
2. To identify the subject and the predicate as the two basic sentence parts
3. To identify the verb and its subject
4. To identify main verbs, helping verbs, and separated parts of a verb
5. To identify the subject in unusual positions, in sentences beginning with *there*, and in imperative sentences
6. To identify direct objects and indirect objects and to understand their functions in sentences
7. To distinguish between action verbs and linking verbs and between predicate words and direct objects
8. To recognize compound sentence parts
9. To identify the four kinds of sentences and to use the proper punctuation for each

Preparing the Students

Before reading the introduction, discuss the comparison of the structure of writing with the structure of a building as presented on page 235. Ask students what is necessary to make a solid building. Emphasize the importance of planning, proper materials, and good craftsmanship. Compare these requirements with those necessary for effective communication. Ask students if they can draw any other parallels between building and writing. Stress the need for completing one's work, whether it is in building or writing. A building without a complete foundation is not usable; a sentence without all of its parts is not effective communication.

Read the introduction on page 235 with the students.

Objective   To distinguish between fragments and complete sentences

Presenting the Lesson   1. Read the definition of a sentence on page 236. Discuss the concept of a complete thought. Point out that in order to be a complete thought, a group of words must tell both *who* or *what* and *what happened*. Explain that a fragment is incomplete because it lacks either the *who* or *what* element or the *what happened* element essential to a complete sentence.

2. Place the following groups of words on the board. Explain that each is a fragment because each expresses only the *who* or *what* element or the *what happened* element, but not both. Have students tell whether each fragment expresses *who* or *what* or *what happened*.

> Won a bronze medal in the Winter Olympics.
> Eleanor and Franklin Roosevelt.
> Is teaching driver-training.
> An after-school job.

3. Assign and discuss the exercises on pages 236 and 237.

Optional Practice   Have students number their papers from 1 to 10. Read the following groups of words aloud. After each group of words is read, students should write *yes* or *no* to indicate whether or not the words express a complete thought.

1. Putting polish on the car's fender.

2. An unidentified flying object.

3. Danny ran the 26-mile marathon.

4. Am always hungry after eating pizza.

5. Everyone in the cafeteria.

6. The bus drivers are on strike.

7. Ran out of ink during the test.

8. Gayle caught a cold.

9. The pitcher threw to second base.

10. I hate the "Incredible Hulk" show!

Extending the Lesson   1. Have students refer to Exercise A on page 236. For each group of words not considered a complete sentence, have students tell why the words do not convey a complete thought. Students should write what is lacking in each item considered incomplete.

2. Have students refer to Exercise B on page 237. For each group of words not considered a complete sentence, students should add words necessary to make a complete sentence. The rewritten complete sentences may be read aloud so that students can compare their own versions with those of classmates.

Part 2 Subjects and Predicates   pp. 237–238

Objective To identify the subject and the predicate as the two basic sentence parts

Presenting the Lesson 1. Review with students the elements necessary to make a complete sentence, as presented in Part 1. Explain that the two elements of a sentence (*who* or *what* and *what happened*) are referred to as the subject and the predicate of the sentence.

2. Read and discuss pages 237 and 238.

3. Write *subject* and *predicate* on the chalkboard to head two columns. Ask student to define both terms.

4. Read the following sentences aloud. For each sentence, ask students to tell you which part of the sentence tells *who* or *what* did something. Write that part under *subject* on the chalkboard. Ask students to tell you which part tells *what is done* or *what happened*. Write that part under *predicate*.

1. Larry made scrambled eggs.

2. The boxing match lasted eight rounds.

3. I want a stereo for my birthday.

4. Betsy babysits for the Kellers.

5. Barbara Walters interviewed Suzanne Sommers.

5. It is suggested that Exercise A on page 238 be done orally with the class. Assign and discuss Exercise B on page 238.

Optional Practice Write the following groups of words on the board. Tell students that the list contains both subjects and predicates. Students should match an appropriate subject and predicate to make a sensible sentence. There is one extra group that will not be used.

1. is helping Anne find a book	6. our garage
2. the puppy	7. spent all of his money
3. the small private plane	8. needs a new roof
4. crashed into a mountain	9. a librarian
5. chewed up my gym shoe	

Extending the Lesson Small groups of students may play this game: 1. Each student writes five complete sentences on a sheet of paper, and then rips another sheet of paper into ten strips, or uses ten index cards. On each strip of paper or card, each student writes one subject or one predicate from his or her sentences. 2. All subject cards are collected, shuffled, and placed in one pile. All predicate cards are handled in the same way. 3. The game begins as one student at a time draws one card from the subject pile and one card from the predicate pile. The resulting sentence, which will no doubt be humorous, should be read aloud. Further humorous combinations can be formed as time permits.

Part 3 **Simple Subjects and Predicates** pp. 239–241

Objective To identify the verb and its subject

Presenting the Lesson 1. Read and discuss page 238. Remind students that until now, they have been dealing with complete subjects and complete predicates. Now they will study the key words within these sentence elements: the simple subject and the simple predicate, or verb.

2. Write the following sentences on the board. Leave a space between each subject and predicate.

1. The early bird	catches the worm.
2. A wild and crazy guy	told some jokes.
3. A small green book	fell off the shelf.
4. Many working people	take this bus.
5. The school nurse	treated my brother.

Ask students to identify the simple subject and simple predicate in each sentence. Underline the subject and verb as they are identified.

3. Read and discuss the bottom of page 239 and page 240.

4. Do Exercise A, page 240–241 orally with the class. Begin each item by asking "What is the verb?" Then, ask *who* or *what* before the verb.

5. Assign and discuss Exercise B on page 241.

Optional Practice Place the following sentences on a worksheet. In each sentence have students underline the verb twice and the subject once.

1. Our new neighbors moved in yesterday.

2. My sister attended the concert downtown.

3. Craig's family bought a snowblower.

4. The workers planted trees and flowers in the park

5. Jack took the shortcut through the alley.

6. The boat in the harbor needs a new sail.

7. My favorite author just wrote a new mystery.

8. This wooden chair always hurts my back.

9. The most unbelievable things happen to Jeremy!

10. Meg took pictures of the basketball game.

Extending the Lesson Place the following sentences on the blackboard or a worksheet. Have students diagram the subject and verb of each sentence, referring to the models on page 240 if necessary.

1. A flock of geese flew over the parking lot.

2. Barbara found some old photographs in the attic.

3. Some football players wear elbow pads.

4. Our car gets thirty miles per gallon of gasoline.

5. Curious fish circled the sunken treasure chest.

Part 4 **The Parts of a Verb**   pp. 241–243

Objective To identify main verbs, helping verbs, and separated parts of a verb

Presenting the Lesson 1. Remind students that the simple predicate (verb) is the key word in the predicate part of the sentence. Tell students that the verb may consist of one word or of several words.
2. Read page 241 and the top of page 242.
3. Put the following pairs of sentences on the board. Have students identify the verbs in each sentence. Point out that some words may be used either as a main verb or as a helping verb.

1. Kerry was our team captain.

2. Gregg was wearing your jacket.

3. This shampoo has lemon in it.

4. Heavy snow has been falling all day.

4. Read and discuss the balance of page 242.

5. Assign and discuss Exercises A and B on pages 242 and 243.

Optional Practice Put the following verbs on the board. Have students write a sentence using each.

1. has been fixing	6. wasn't trying
2. doesn't know	7. will be
3. am	8. hasn't written
4. am reading	9. has
5. could have been eating	10. couldn't be seen

Extending the Lesson Have students complete one of the following exercises, depending upon their writing abilities and/or the accessibility of newspapers and magazines.

a. Students should write a one-page summary of the plot of a fa-favorite TV show or movie. After the page is written neatly, students should use a red pen to underline all verbs. In sentences in which both helping verbs and main verbs appear, the main verb should be circled as well as underlined.

b. Students should clip out a news story or magazine column. Using a red pen, students should underline all verbs. In sentences in which both helping verbs and main verbs appear, the main verb should be circled as well as underlined.

Part 5 **Subjects in Unusual Positions** pp. 243–247

Objective To identify the subject in unusual positions, in sentences beginning with *there*, and in imperative sentences

Presenting the Lesson 1. Read and discuss page 243. Stress that even when the subject does not come before the verb, the subject is located by first finding the verb and then asking *who* or *what* before the verb.

2. Place the following sentence pairs on the board.

No driver is on the bus.   A printed answer isn't there.
There is no driver on the bus.   There isn't a printed answer.

The books you need are there.
There are the books you need.

Have students find the subject in the first sentence in each pair. Point out that the second sentence of each pair has exactly the same meaning. The subject and verb are identical—but have been reversed in order. Have students find the subject in the second sentence of each pair.

3. Read and discuss page 244.
4. Do Exercise A on page 244 orally with the class.
5. Assign and discuss Exercise B on page 245.
6. Read and discuss pages 245–246.
7. Assign and discuss Exercises A and B on page 247.

Optional Practice   Have students rewrite the following sentences with the subject in a different position. After sentences are rewritten, students should underline the verb twice and the subject once.

1. A swarm of bees flew through the field.
2. Here are the books for your sister.
3. Slowly came the final tally.
4. The army's defeat was here.
5. The deer ran into the forest.

Extending the Lesson   Have students diagram the following sentences. Instruct students to review examples of diagrams on pages 244 and 246.

1. Does David know about our plans?
2. Put your boots by the door.
3. Around my neck hung the medal.
4. Here are the notes from class.
5. There must be an escape hatch.

Part 6   **Objects of Verbs**   pp. 247–251

Objective   To identify direct objects and indirect objects and to understand their functions

Presenting the Lesson   1. Read pages 247–248.
2. Stress that a direct object completes the meaning of the sentence by telling *what* or *whom* after the verb.
3. Place the following sentences on the board. Ask students which

are complete and which need objects to complete the action of their verbs.

1. The stop sign blew down.
2. Mr. Miller cut down.
3. Gloria is waiting.
4. The children are bringing.
5. The old Buick needs.

As students identify sentences 2, 4, and 5 as needing objects, guide them to locate the verb and then to ask *what* or *whom*. Ask students for suggestions to complete sentences 2, 4, and 5.

4. Point out the difference between direct objects and words which tell *how, where, when,* or *to what extent*.

5. Assign and discuss the exercise on page 249.

6. Read page 249. Emphasize these points:

1. Indirect objects appear only in sentences with direct objects.
2. The indirect object always appears before the direct object.
3. Indirect objects answer the questions *to whom* or *for whom* or *to what* or *for what* after the verb.
4. Indirect objects are not found after the words *to* or *for*.

7. Place these sentences on the board. Have students make three columns on their papers headed *Verb, Direct Object,* and *Indirect Object*. Have students fill in the columns with the correct words in each sentence. Not every sentence will contain all three parts.

1. Sandy told me her good news.
2. You can deliver the papers tomorrow.
3. Paul asked Ms. Riggs a question.
4. She answered it quickly.
5. Perfume gives me a horrible rash.

8. Assign and discuss Exercises A and B on page 250.

Extending the Lesson   For students who understand the function of objects, assign the following exercise:

Expand the sentences below by making the additions indicated. Write a new sentence for each addition.

1. Natalie Cole sang.
   a. add a direct object
   b. add an indirect object and a direct object
2. Artie is driving.
   a. add a direct object
3. Maria was reading.
   a. add a direct object
   b. add an indirect object and a direct object
4. Julia Child cooked.
   a. add a direct object
5. Janice wrote.
   a. add a direct object
   b. add an indirect object and a direct object

Part 7 **Linking Verbs and Predicate Words**
pp. 251–253

Objective   To distinguish between action verbs and linking verbs and between predicate words and direct objects

Presenting the Lesson   1. Remind the class that direct and indirect objects help complete the action of the verb. All of the verbs dealt with in Part 6 were action verbs. Their action was received or complemented by a direct object or by an indirect object and a direct object. Now, inform students that they will learn about different kinds of verbs, called *linking verbs*. Explain that linking verbs do not express action. Rather, they tell of a state of being.

2. Read and discuss page 251 and the top of page 252. Make certain that students are familiar with all of the forms of *be* on page 251, including those used with helping verbs. Make certain that students are familiar with all of the other common linking verbs on page 252.

3. Stress that the "link" in linking verbs is between the subject and the predicate word. Point out that the predicate word tells something about the subject.

4. Place the following sentences on the chalkboard:

1. Marla is the co-captain.
2. Dr. Nold was a fine dentist.

3. The bicycle must be my gift.

4. The photographs look beautiful.

5. Dad sounded worried on the phone.

Using one sentence at a time, ask students to identify the verb. Underline the verb on the chalkboard as it is identified. Ask students to identify the subject. Draw a circle around the subject. Ask students to identify a word which tells about the subject. Circle the predicate word. Draw an arrow from the predicate word to the subject. Stress that the link is between the predicate word and the subject. In sentences 1–3, the predicate word renames the subject. In sentences 4 and 5, the predicate word describes the subject.

5. Read pages 252 and 253. Use the following sentences to reinforce understanding of the difference between predicate words and direct objects.

The waiter dropped the food.
The waiter was clumsy.

Bette Midler won a Grammy award.
Bette Midler is a singer.

Dracula bit the victim's neck.
Dracula is my favorite movie.

In each pair of sentences, point out that the first sentence contains an action verb which has its action completed by a direct object. Remind students that the direct object answers *what* or *whom* after the verb. Point out that the second sentence in each pair contains a linking verb. Ask students what words are linked in each sentence.

6. Assign and discuss Exercise A on page 253. Students who have difficulty with this exercise should be assigned the exercise in the Optional Practice below before going on to Exercise B.

7. Assign and discuss Exercise B on page 253.

Optional Practice   Have students write sentences using each of the following linking verbs. In their completed sentences, students should underline the verb, circle the subject, circle the predicate word, and draw an arrow from the predicate word to the subject.

1. are becoming	5. will be	9. seemed
2. is	6. would have been	10. has been
3. tasted	7. appears	
4. are	8. felt	

Extending the Lesson   Place these sentences on a worksheet, leaving plenty of space between sentences. Have students do the following for each sentence.

1. Locate the verb and underline it twice.
2. Mark *AV* over each action verb. Mark *LV* over each linking verb.
3. Circle all objects and predicate words.
4. Mark *DO* over each direct object. Mark *PW* over each predicate word.

   1. Eric wore a Superman costume for Halloween.
   2. The cake seemed stale.
   3. The Johnsons bought the ranch in Texas.
   4. Richard Nixon was President from 1969 to 1974.
   5. The car windows are dirty.
   6. Jason seems restless today.
   7. A cotton shirt feels cool on a warm day.
   8. Claude tuned his guitar.
   9. That horse will be a winner.
   10. The pilot should have been more careful.

Part 8   Compound Sentence Parts   pp. 254–255

Objective   To recognize compound sentence parts

Presenting the Lesson   1. Review the sentence parts covered thus far: subject, verb, direct object, indirect object, and predicate word.
   2. Place the following sentences on the board. Ask students to identify the part indicated in parentheses.

   1. Gilda and Jane read the news report. (subject)
   2. Jerry cut and sanded the wood. (verb)
   3. Lindsay plays both piano and violin. (direct object)
   4. The dean gave Fran and me a lecture. (indirect object)
   5. Today has been cold and rainy. (predicate word)

Point out how each sentence element identified consists of two parts.
   3. Read and discuss page 254.
   4. Do Exercise A on page 255 orally with the class.

5. For students who need more practice in identifying compound sentence parts, assign the exercise in the Optional Practice.

6. Assign and discuss Exercise B on page 255.

Optional Practice   Place the following exercise on a worksheet. Ask students to find the compound parts in the following sentences. Students should tell whether the compound parts are compound subjects, compound verbs, compound objects, or compound predicate words.

1. Lisa and Louis are twins.
2. Mr. Haines has become rich and famous.
3. We picked some corn and tomatoes from our garden.
4. Red Cross helpers fed and clothed the victims.
5. The elm tree grew tall and stately over the years.
6. Tennis and basketball are good exercise.
7. Everyone should bring suits, towels, and lunch to the beach.
8. Betsy likes sports and music.
9. Barry stacked the logs and built a fire.
10. The director gave Emily and Adam their cues.

Extending the Lesson   Place the following partial sentences on the board or on a worksheet. Have students complete the sentences with the compound parts indicated.

1. _____ were destroyed in the fire. (compound subject)
2. John _____ the door. (compound verb)
3. Terry opened _____. (compound direct object)
4. The workers _____ the house. (compound verb)
5. _____ are delicious foods. (compound subject)

Part 9   **Kinds of Sentences**   pp. 256–257

Objective   To identify the four kinds of sentences and to use the proper punctuation for each

Presenting the Lesson   1. Read and discuss page 256. Point out that while the names of the four types of sentences may sound difficult, students have encountered all four types of sentences in this section.

2. Stress the importance of purpose in determining sentence type.

3. Assign Exercises A and B on page 257.

Optional Practice Have students identify the type of sentence for each of the following sentences and add proper end punctuation.

1. Have you ever gone deep sea fishing
2. You must never go near the water
3. The sermon was about charity
4. What fun we had at the beach
5. What will we eat for lunch
6. Plan to watch *Laverne and Shirley* tonight
7. My family went camping last weekend
8. Is that smog or smoke
9. Fans, get your scorecards ready
10. Help

Extending the Lesson Have students write sentences of the type indicated, using the subjects and verbs given.

1. declarative   subject—spaghetti
2. interrogative   subject—puppies
3. exclamatory   verb—crashed
4. imperative   verb—stop
5. imperative   verb—listen

Review

p. 258

You may use the review on page 258 either as a checkup or for additional practice.

Using Complete Sentences
Pages 259–264

Objectives

1. To avoid and correct sentence fragments
2. To avoid and correct run-on sentences

Preparing the Students

Ask students if they have ever had the experience of listening to someone who is very excited tell a story. The person rushes his ideas together and leaves out important details so that you cannot follow the story. You understand all of the words, but the ideas don't always make sense to you.

Explain that this is also a frequent problem in writing; if the writer is not careful in creating sentences, a reader may not be able to understand his ideas.

Tell students that this chapter will point out two common problems in writing.

Read the introduction on page 259. Remind students that sentences are the foundation on which good writing rests. Avoiding fragments and run-ons will help students make their writing foundation solid.

Part 1 **Avoiding Sentence Fragments** pp. 260–262

Objective To avoid and correct sentence fragments

Presenting the Lesson 1. Ask students to define a fragment as used in these examples:

> Only a fragment of the picture could be seen.
> Fragments of cloth were scattered on the floor.
> The child could recall only fragments of his dream.

Lead the class to understand that fragments are bits and pieces. They belong to a larger whole and are incomplete by themselves. Fragments don't convey a whole picture or a whole story.

Explain that sometimes, even though a writer has a complete idea in his mind, he may write in fragments because he doesn't take the time to express his ideas completely. To communicate effectively, a good writer must avoid fragments.

2. Read and discuss page 260, paying careful attention to examples of fragments and their corrections.

3. Put these fragments on the board. Ask students whether the *subject* or the *verb* is missing. Have students supply missing elements to make complete sentences.

1. The doctor and nurse.

2. Fell down from its nest.

3. Danced all night at the disco.

4. Leah, the main character in the book.

5. Hired Yvette Simms for the job.

4. Read and discuss the top of page 261. Point out that sometimes the writer has written all of the parts he needs to express a complete thought, but he has punctuated these parts incorrectly and thus created fragments.

5. Put these sentences and fragments on the board. Analyze each with the class, determining which part is a fragment and correcting the error in punctuation to eliminate the fragment.

1. It was noisy in the library. With all the students there.

2. We enjoyed the movie. Especially the special effects.

3. Try to lift the cartons. Of heavy books. Without straining your back.

4. By New Year's. I must lose five pounds.

5. After the election. The mayor left town.

6. Assign and discuss Exercises A and B on pages 261–262.

Optional Practice   Put the following sentences and fragments on a worksheet or on the blackboard. Have students identify which are fragments and rewrite them as complete sentences.

1. Muhammad Ali retired from boxing. After winning the fight with Leon Spinx.

2. A six-car pileup on the expressway.

3. Most clothing goes on sale. After Christmas and after the Fourth of July.

4. Laura had her braces taken off. She looks wonderful.

5. Blanca, our white German shepherd puppy.

Objective To avoid and correct run-on sentences

Presenting the Lesson 1. Read and discuss page 262. Stress that the problem in run-on sentences is that the writer runs together two separate, complete thoughts. Run-ons cause confusion because they don't allow the reader to form his ideas in a logical way. When proper punctuation is missing, the reader doesn't have the necessary guides for making sense of the words. He doesn't know where one idea ends and another begins.

2. Do Exercise A on pages 262–263 orally with the class. After breaking each run-on into two sentences, determine whether each resulting sentence is complete. Identify the subject and the verb in each sentence.

3. Assign and discuss Exercise B on page 263.

Optional Practice Put the following sentences on the board. Have students determine which are run-ons. Have students correct and rewrite run-on sentences.

1. The days are getting shorter, we rode home in the dark.

2. Mr. Rogers is still on television, he was on when I was a little kid.

3. Nancy brought grapes and peaches don't they look delicious?

4. Before painting the posters, Carl put on a smock.

5. A train derailed near St. Louis no one was hurt, the track was closed for the rest of the day.

Extending the Lesson For students who are skilled at identifying complete sentence structures and correcting fragments and run-ons, you might want to discuss alternate ways of correcting run-ons. Use the following examples to show that run-ons need not always be broken into two separate sentences.

Run-on:	Christopher Reeve starred in *Superman* he is still not a well known actor.
Correct:	Christopher Reeve starred in *Superman*, but he is still not a well known actor.
Run-on:	Our picnic was ruined it rained.
Correct:	Our picnic was ruined because it rained.

Run-on:	We got new tires I never realized how bad the old ones were.
Correct:	Until we got new tires, I never realized how bad the old ones were.

Have students correct the following run-ons in ways other than by creating two separate sentences.

1. I read the whole story, I didn't understand all of it.
2. Larry bought a tape deck for his car now he listens to music when he drives.
3. The Highway Patrol stopped the van, one of its headlights was out.
4. You didn't water the plant enough it died.
5. Mike lifts weights every day, he is really very strong.

Review

p. 264

You may use the review on page 264 either as a checkup or for additional practice.

Using Nouns

Pages 265–279

Objectives

1. To understand the concept of a noun and to identify nouns in sentences
2. To distinguish between common nouns and proper nouns
3. To identify nouns used as subjects, direct objects, indirect objects, and predicate nouns
4. To form the plural of nouns correctly
5. To form and use possessive nouns correctly

Preparing the Students

Ask students if any of them have baby brothers or sisters, or are familiar with any very small children. Ask those who have had experience with youngsters who are just beginning to talk what the first words the youngsters said were. List on the board the words recalled. Most words will relate to people (DaDa, Mama), things (cookie, doll), and possibly places (bed, park). Ask students what all of these words have in common. Students should recognize that all are names.

Explain that one of the most basic elements of language is the noun, which names people, places, and things.

Tell students that the next section in the text will teach them about an important group of words: nouns.

Read the introduction on page 265 with students.

Part 1 **What Are Nouns?**   pp. 266–267

Objectives   1. To understand the concept of a noun
2. To identify nouns in sentences
3. To distinguish between common nouns and proper nouns

Presenting the Lesson   1. Read the top of page 266. Pay special attention to examples of persons, places, and things.

2. Place the three headings *Persons, Places,* and *Things* on the blackboard to form three columns. Ask students to volunteer names of persons, places, and things to be listed under each heading. Try to elicit examples of abstract nouns, such as the text examples of *loyalty* and *love.*

3. Assign and discuss the exercise on page 266.

4. Read pages 266–267 dealing with proper nouns and common nouns, paying special attention to examples on page 267. Point out capitalization of proper nouns in examples.

5. Place the following common nouns on the board. Ask students to give at least five examples of proper nouns for each.

> 1. city   2. street   3. actor   4. automobile   5. athlete

6. Assign and discuss Exercises A and B on page 267.

Optional Practice   Put the following exercise on a worksheet:
Make three columns below this paragraph, using the headings (1) Names of Persons (2) Names of Places (3) Names of Things.

Under the proper heading, list each noun in the following paragraph. Put an asterisk (*) before each proper noun.

Australia is both an island and a continent that lies south of the equator. Queen Elizabeth II of Great Britain is also the Queen of Australia. Sydney is the largest city and Canberra is the capital of Australia. Life in Australia is much like life in the United States and Canada. Australians speak English, but with a different accent from that spoken by Americans or Canadians. Australia is an important farming and industrial country. It is the leading producer of bauxite, sheep, and wool. Australia also raises much beef and wheat and produces much copper, gold, and iron.

Extending the Lesson Have students play the following "Jeopardy" game. Each answer at the left below must be solved by a student's offering a question which centers around a noun. Students may make up their own questions as well. Students should be able to tell whether their nouns are common nouns or proper nouns.

Example: Answer—2,000 pounds | Question—What is a ton?

1. the daughter of Pat Boone   (Who is Debby Boone?)
2. the home state of
Ted Kennedy   (What is Massachusetts?)
3. the shape of a stop sign   (What is an octagon?)
4. Miss Piggie and Kermit   (What are Muppets?)
5. the seed of an oak tree   (What is an acorn?)
6. author of *Romeo and Juliet*   (Who is Shakespeare?)
7. decides if a pitch is a ball or
a strike   (What is an umpire?)
8. came from the planet Ork   (Who is Mork?)
9. girl in Wizard of Oz   (Who is Dorothy?)
10. animals Little Bo Peep lost   (What are sheep?)

Part 2 **How Are Nouns Used?** pp. 268–274

Objective To identify nouns used as subjects, direct objects, indirect objects, and predicate nouns

Presenting the Lesson This part may be divided into four separate lessons: Nouns Used as Subjects (steps 1–3), Nouns Used as Direct Objects (steps 4–6), Noun Used as Indirect Objects (steps 7–9), and Nouns Used as Predicate Nouns (steps 10–12).

1. Read and discuss page 268, carefully analyzing examples. Point out that nouns used as subjects may be names of people—either specific individuals (*trainer, Maria, Tyrone*) or groups (*team*). Both common nouns and proper nouns may be used as subjects. Point out that nouns used as subjects may also be names of places or things, as in these examples:

1. San Francisco was jolted by an earthquake.
2. The library closes at 5:00.
3. The kite is stuck in a tree.
4. Your loyalty pleases me.
5. Dishonesty cannot be tolerated.

2. Do Exercise A on page 268 orally with the class. Discuss whether the subjects are common nouns or proper nouns. Point out the compound subject in number 7. Point out that the subject is not right next to the verb in number 9.

3. Assign and discuss Exercise B on page 269.

4. Read and discuss page 269 and the top of page 270. Remind students that in order to find the direct object, they should locate the verb first and then ask *what* or *whom* immediately after the verb.

5. Do Exercise A on page 270 orally with the class.

6. Assign and discuss Exercise B on page 270.

7. Read and discuss page 271. Point out that when the words *to* or *for* appear in the sentence, the word which follows them is not an indirect object. Example: Eduardo gave a lottery ticket to me.

8. Do Exercise A on page 272 orally with the class. If time permits, identify subject, verb, direct object, and indirect object for each sentence.

9. Assign and discuss Exercise B on page 272.

10. Read the bottom of page 272 and page 273. Stress that a predicate noun renames the subject.

11. Do Exercise A on page 273 orally with the class.

12. Assign and discuss Exercise B on page 274.

Optional Practice Place the following sentences on the board or on a worksheet. Have students underline all nouns. Above each noun, have students write *s* (subject), *do* (direct object), *io* (indirect object), or *pn* (predicate noun) to indicate the way each noun is used in the sentences.

1. "M.A.S.H." is my favorite program.
2. Batman gave Robin a special assignment.
3. Honda and Kawasaki make fine cycles.
4. The cups and saucers are dirty.
5. This car needs new plugs and points.
6. Tardiness and absence have been major problems.
7. The farmer planted corn, peas, and beans.
8. Both the House and the Senate approved the bill.
9. Cindy sent many friends and relatives her pictures.
10. Spend the money for food and clothing.

Extending the Lesson For students who can successfully identify nouns and label them as to function, some practice in diagramming would be appropriate. For diagramming practice, five sentences each may be drawn from the following exercises: Exercise B, page 270, Exercise B, page 272, Exercise B, page 274.

Part 3 **Forming the Plural of Nouns** pp. 274–276

Objective To form the plural of nouns correctly

Presenting the Lesson 1. Read pages 274 and 275. Go over rules for forming plurals carefully, especially noting examples. Ask students for additional examples for each rule.
2. Assign and discuss Exercise A on page 276.
3. Assign and discuss Exercise B on page 276.

Optional Practice Have students copy the following sentences using the plural form of the noun in parentheses. Dictionaries may be used if necessary.

1. The (paintbrush) were too stiff to use.
2. After he broke his leg, Dan used (crutch) for one month.
3. The (piano) and (cello) played together.
4. Helen put (mango) in the fruit salad.
5. War (hero) are given medals.

6. Yellow (daisy) grow outside our windows.

7. The lawyer typed her own (brief).

8. The (fish) were biting; Meg caught several (trout).

9. The dentist wants to pull my wisdom (tooth).

10. A flock of (goose) flew high overhead.

Part 4 **Forming the Possessive of Nouns**   pp. 276–278

Objectives   1. To understand the concept of possessive nouns
2. To form and use possessive nouns correctly

Presenting the Lesson   1. Read and discuss pages 276–277. Go over rules for forming possessives carefully, especially noting examples. Ask students for additional examples for each rule.
2. Do Exercise A on page 277 with the class. Send four volunteers to the board. Each student should do five items so that the class can see properly written possessives.
3. Assign and discuss Exercise B on page 278.
4. Assign and discuss Exercise C on page 278.

Optional Practice   Have students divide their papers into four columns, labeled *Singular, Plural, Singular Possessive,* and *Plural Possessive*. Students should copy the following nouns in the column labeled *Singular*. Students should then fill in the other three columns for each word.

1. officer	5. lady	9. baby
2. city	6. girl	10. dancer
3. day	7. winner	
4. citizen	8. monkey	

Extending the Lesson   Have students use each of the following nouns in sentences. Students should be able to identify the nouns they use as either singular, plural, singular possessive, or plural possessive.

1. Melanie's	5. dress	9. heroes'
2. Mondays	6. women's	10. Betty's
3. Friday's	7. New York's	
4. The Grays'	8. soprano's	

You may use the review on page 279 either as a checkup or for additional practice.

Using Pronouns

Pages 280–301

Objectives

1. To understand the concept of the pronoun
2. To recognize the singular and plural personal pronouns
3. To recognize and use personal pronouns in the subject form, object form, and possessive form
4. To use the correct pronoun in compound sentence parts
5. To use pronouns that agree with their antecedents in number
6. To form compound personal pronouns and to use them correctly
7. To use demonstrative pronouns correctly
8. To recognize and use interrogative pronouns correctly
9. To distinguish between singular and plural indefinite pronouns
10. To check for agreement in number between indefinite pronouns and their verbs or other possessive pronouns that refer to them
11. To use pronouns correctly in situations that often cause problems:
    1) possessive pronouns and contractions   2) *who* and *whom*
    3) *we* and *us*   4) *them* and *those*

Preparing the Students

Ask students if the following sentence makes complete sense: "It looks good on her; she should buy it." Most likely, students will respond that they don't know what the sentence is trying to say. They will want to know who *she* is and what *it* is.

Now ask students if this sentence is more complete: "The floppy hat looks good on Gina; she should buy it."

Students will see that once the nouns *hat* and *Gina* are presented, the use of *it* and *she* becomes acceptable. Explain that *it* and *she* are pronouns.

Ask students if the following sentence is as acceptable as the one read previously: "The floppy hat looks good on Gina; Gina should buy the floppy hat."

Most likely students will suggest that it is unnecessary to repeat the nouns in such close proximity. Explain that pronouns are a very useful part of speech because they help avoid repetition by taking the place of nouns.

Read and discuss the introduction on page 280.

Part 1 **Personal Pronouns**   pp. 281–282

Objectives   1. To understand the concept of the pronoun
2. To recognize the singular and plural personal pronouns

Presenting the Lesson   1. Read page 281. Carefully study examples of pronouns used in the three situations illustrated. Go over the list of singular and plural personal pronouns at the bottom of page 281.
2. Using the list of pronouns at the bottom of page 281, go around the class and have each student use one pronoun in a sentence.
3. Assign and discuss Exercises A and B on page 282.

Optional Practice   Have students fill the blanks in the following sentences with pronouns. Students should identify the noun to which each pronoun refers.

  1. The seniors are making plans for _____ prom.

     _____ are having _____ at a hotel downtown.

  2. Geri told _____ boss that _____ had to leave early.

  3. Scott and Ralph took _____ brothers with _____
     to the park.

  4. All teenagers want to be treated like adults; give

     _____ a chance so _____ can show _____
     best sides.

Part 2 **The Forms of Pronouns**   pp. 283–287

Objective   To recognize and use personal pronouns in the subject form, object form, and possessive form

Presenting the Lesson 1. Ask students to supply pronouns in the following sentence:

> The teacher asked Sharon if (she) would put (her) diagram on the board, since (hers) was the best in the class.

After writing *she, her,* and *hers* on the board, ask students to what noun all three pronouns refer. Stress that although all three refer to *Sharon,* they are in different forms. Explain that pronouns change form according to the ways in which they are used.

2. Read page 283.

3. Do the exercise on pages 283 and 284. Analyze each pronoun to determine if it is in the subject, object, or possessive form. Students should try to make this determination in terms of the pronoun's function in the sentence, and then check with the chart on page 283.

4. Read page 284 and the top of 285. Remind students that pronouns can be used anywhere a noun can be used. Two common uses of nouns are as subjects and as predicate nouns. Pronouns used in both of these ways have the same form. Emphasize that pronouns used as subjects and pronouns used as predicate pronouns have the same form. Carefully examine and discuss examples.

5. Read page 285 and the top of 286. Review direct objects and indirect objects with students, referring to pages 247–249 and 269–272 as necessary.

6. Have students supply the correct object pronoun in these sentences. Have students tell whether the pronoun is used as direct object, indirect object, or object of the preposition.

> I ordered a deluxe cheeseburger. The waitress served
>
> _____ to _____. She forgot to bring _____ the french
>
> fries and cole slaw. I wanted _____, so I called her back.

7. Read page 286. Carefully study examples. Point out that possessive pronouns alone can be used in the five ways nouns can be used.

8. Have students supply the correct possessive pronouns in these sentences. Have students tell whether the possessive pronoun used tells about a noun, or is used by itself as subject, direct object, object of the preposition, indirect object, or predicate pronoun.

1. We gave our dog _____ bath.

2. The winners received cash. I spent _____ right away.

3. Fran entered the art show; the best entry was _____.

4. Your turn will come after _____.

5. Come on, give _____ a break.

6. Joyce lost her favorite scarf. _____ found _____ in the yard.

9. Do Exercise A on pages 286–287 orally with the class.

10. Assign and discuss Exercises B and C on page 287.

Optional Practice Have students rewrite the following sentences, substituting pronouns for the underlined nouns.

1. The students wrote *the students'* assignment just as *the students'* teacher had told *the students* to do.

2. The voters re-elected the Senator. *The voters* liked *the Senator* better than *the Senator's* opponents. *The voters* felt that the best candidate was *the Senator*.

3. The group performed a folk song as *the group's* final number. *We fans* cheered for *the group* so loudly that *the group* sang *us fans* an encore.

Part 3 **Pronouns in Compound Sentence Parts**
pp. 288–289

Objective To use the correct pronoun form in compound sentence parts

Presenting the Lesson 1. Read page 288. Remind students that they have already dealt with compound parts of sentences (Part 8, Section 1). Tell them that there are two ways to check to make sure that the correct form of a pronoun is used in a compound sentence part. One way, as suggested on page 288, is to read the sentence with just the pronoun in question, eliminating the other noun or pronoun. Another way to decide which form of the pronoun to use is to determine whether the pronoun in question is used as a subject or as an object. If it is used as a subject, the subject form should be used (refer students to the list on page 284). If the pronoun is used as an object, the object form should be used (refer students to the list on page 285).

2. Assign and discuss Exercises A and B on page 289.

Optional Practice Have students complete the following exercise, choosing the right pronoun from the parentheses in each sentence.

110

1. The twins and (I, me) are training for the relay race.
2. An invitation to Eric and (he, him) arrived today.
3. The priest blessed (they, them) and (we, us).
4. The secret must be kept between you and (I, me).
5. The monitors were freshmen and (we, us).
6. Gregory and (he, him) are the best guards.
7. Call your parents and (they, them) when you get to Cleveland.
8. Ryan and (I, me) went to camp together.
9. (She, Her) and her sister look very much alike.
10. There is no difference between (they, them) and the sale items.

Extending the Lesson For the students who can correctly choose pronoun forms as in Exercise A and the Optional Practice, and correct errors in form as in Exercise B, the following exercise may be beneficial. Have students return to Exercise A, Exercise B, or the Optional Practice and state in what form the correct pronoun appears. If it is in subject form, students should tell if it functions as a subject or a predicate pronoun. If it is in object form, students should tell if it is used as a direct object, an indirect object, or an object of the preposition.

Part 4 **Pronouns and Antecedents**   pp. 289–291

Objective To use pronouns that agree with their antecedents in number

Presenting the Lesson 1. Read pages 289–290. Make certain that students understand the definitions of *antecedent*, *number*, and *agree*.

2. Some analysis of the word *antecedent* may help students understand this concept. Explain the Latin derivation: *ante-* = before, *cede* = go or yield. An antecedent is that which goes before. Related words which will help illustrate the meaning of antecedent are: *antedate* (dated before), *anteroom* (room before, hallway), *anterior* (front), *precede* (go before), and *recede* (go back).

3. Assign and discuss Exercises A and B on pages 290 and 291.

Extending the Lesson Have students who can successfully identify antecedents and determine if the antecedent is singular or plural do the following exercise.

Have students choose a pronoun from those given in parentheses that will agree in number with its antecedent.

1. Both birds in the nest called for (his, their) mother.
2. Tie the ribbons on each box, but don't cut (it, them).
3. A nurse must keep (his or her, their) uniform clean.
4. Russell and Scott have (their, his) own skis.
5. Dad's shirt sleeves are too long, so he rolls (it, them) up.
6. Three doctors from the hospital offered (his, their) help.
7. The drapes burst into flames after the candle touched (it, them).
8. The mechanics used (his or her, their) own tools.
9. The needles on the tree are falling from (its, their) branches.
10. Every student should do (his or her, their) best.

Part 5 **Compound Personal Pronouns**   pp. 291–292

Objective   To form compound personal pronouns and to use them correctly

Presenting the Lesson   1. Read page 291, studying the list of compound personal pronouns and examples of their use.

2. Assign and discuss Exercises A and B on page 292. Be sure students read the seventh sentence in Exercise B carefully—the plural *yourselves* is called for because *you both* is plural.

Extending the Lesson   Have students write sentences using each of the eight compound personal pronouns on page 291. Have students underline each compound personal pronoun and underline the noun or pronoun to which it refers.

Part 6 **Demonstrative Pronouns**   pp. 292–293

Objective   To use demonstrative pronouns correctly

Presenting the Lesson   1. Read page 292 and the top of page 293. Stress that to be considered a demonstrative pronoun, the word *this, that, these,* or *those* must be used by itself and not before another noun.

This is my suitcase. (demonstrative pronoun)
This suitcase is mine. (adjective)

2. Assign and discuss the exercise on page 293. For items over which there is confusion, discuss whether the thing referred to is near or far.

Part 7 **Interrogative Pronouns** pp. 293–294

Objective To recognize and use interrogative pronouns correctly

Presenting the Lesson 1. Read page 293. Make certain that students can relate the concept of interrogative pronouns to the explanation of interrogative sentences on page 256. Point out that demonstrative pronouns may appear in interrogative sentences, as in these examples:

Can *those* be your cousins?
Is *this* a fungus?
Has *that* spilled already?

Interrogative pronouns usually appear as the first word in a sentence, as in these examples:

Who invited so many people?
What is your problem?

Interrogative pronouns may follow the preposition *to, for,* or *from,* as in these examples:

From *whom* did you borrow the camera?
For *what* are you being punished?

2. Assign and discuss the exercise on page 293 and 294.

Optional Practice Have students supply appropriate demonstrative or interrogative pronouns in the following sentences.

1. _____ came in the back door?
2. _____ can't be happening to me!
3. To _____ should I deliver _____?
4. Is _____ the horse you usually ride?
5. _____ are the size 12 shoes?
6. For _____ did the audience applaud loudly?

7. _____ is a brilliant idea, Sally.

8. _____ are we playing against?

9. _____ were the happiest days of my vacation.

10. _____ of the restaurants should we choose?

Part 8 Indefinite Pronouns

pp. 294–296

Objectives 1. To distinguish between singular and plural indefinite pronouns

2. To check for agreement in number between indefinite pronouns and their verbs and other possessive pronouns that refer to them

Presenting the Lesson 1. Read pages 294 and 295. Stress that all of the indefinite pronouns in the first list are always singular. Only the four indefinite pronouns in the second list are always plural. To determine if *all, some,* or *none* are singular or plural, students must decide whether they are meant to be singular or plural in individual sentences. Point out that in all of the examples on pages 294 and 295, not only do indefinite pronouns agree in number with possessive pronouns, but they also agree with their verbs: everyone *has*, not everyone *have*. Stress that *his or her* is the acceptable reference to both sexes. *Their* should only be used to indicate a plural.

2. Assign Exercise A on page 295. Go over answers and have students locate other possessive pronouns in each sentence and check for agreement in number.

3. Assign and discuss Exercise B on page 295. Point out that in numbers 3, 7, 9, and 10, the subject of the sentence is the indefinite pronoun, not the noun in the prepositional phrase (refer to page 285 in Handbook Section 7).

4. Assign and discuss Exercise C. Again, caution students that the subject of the sentence is never found in a prepositional phrase.

Optional Practice Have students write sentences using the following indefinite pronouns. Students should make sure verbs and any possessive pronouns agree in number with the indefinite pronoun.

1. anyone	5. all	9. everyone
2. none	6. both	10. few
3. no one	7. some	
4. several	8. someone	

Extending the Lesson   Have students correct errors in the following sentences and explain why the correction is needed.

1. Neither of the boys have had their lunch.
2. Each of our grandparents have their own cars.
3. Somebody left their notebook behind.
4. Another of the flowers have lost their petals.
5. Some of the cars couldn't get out of its parking spaces.

Part 9 **Special Pronoun Problems**   pp. 296–300

Objective   To use pronouns correctly in situations that often cause problems: 1) possessive pronouns and contractions 2) *who* and *whom* 3) *we* and *us* 4) *them* and *those*

Presenting the Lesson   1. Read page 297. Study the five examples. Analyze each example to point out whether the correctly used word is a possessive pronoun or a contraction. In the third and fourth examples, point out that both the contraction and the possessive pronoun are used.

2. Assign and discuss Exercise A on page 297. Have students specify whether the correct choice is a contraction or a possessive pronoun.

3. Assign and discuss Exercise B on pages 297–298.

4. Read page 298. Carefully analyze examples. Explain that in questions such as "Whom did you meet?" *whom* is the direct object of the verb *did meet*. Even though *whom* comes before the verb, it is not the subject of the verb. Remind students that in order to form questions (interrogative sentences) natural word order is changed; the sentence begins with the interrogative pronoun.

5. Assign and discuss Exercises A and B on pages 298 and 299. Have students tell whether the correct pronoun is used as a subject or an object.

6. Read pages 299–300. Carefully analyze examples.

7. Do Exercise A on page 300 orally with the class. Explain that *we* is always used as a subject, and *us* is always used as an object. Analyze each sentence to determine whether the correct answer is used as a subject or an object, or whether the correct answer is an adjective. Point out that it is correct to say "We need *them*," when *them* is the direct object of the verb *need*. It is necessary to say "We

115

need *those* applications," because *those* is an adjective describing *applications*.

8. Assign and discuss Exercise B on page 300.

Optional Practice Have students fill the blanks in the following sentences with *it's, they're, its, their, who, we boys, you're, who's, your, whose, whom, us boys,* or *those.*

1. The flag flapped against _____ pole.
2. Can you see _____ running?
3. _____ car is blocking our driveway.
4. _____ plans to enter the contest?
5. Do you like _____ cupcakes?
6. _____ making all that noise?
7. _____ will be the winner?
8. Mr. Gibbs gave _____ quite a workout.
9. To _____ is the check made payable?
10. _____ playing our song on _____ record player.

Review

p. 301

You may use the review on page 301 either as a checkup or for additional practice.

Using Verbs

Pages 302–323

Objectives

1. To identify verbs as either action verbs or linking verbs
2. To differentiate between transitive and intransitive verbs
3. To identify main verbs, helping verbs, and separated verb parts
4. To understand the concept of verb tense

5. To use verbs in the simple tenses and the perfect tenses

6. To identify and form the principal parts of regular verbs

7. To use the principal parts of irregular verbs correctly

8. To use the principal parts of troublesome pairs of verbs correctly: *learn* and *teach*, *let* and *leave*, *lie* and *lay*, *may* and *can*, *rise* and *raise*, *sit* and *set*

Preparing the Students

Tell students that you are going to read them three sentences about a fire:

> The fire crackled merrily in the fireplace.
> The fire raged out of control through the forest.
> The fire smoldered silently in the cushions of the couch.

Ask students how the three sentences create different images of a fire. The different actions are conveyed by three specific verbs. Remind students that verbs are essential components of complete sentences. Verbs are the moving power, or the motor of a sentence.

Read the introduction on page 302.

Part 1 **What Are Verbs?** pp. 303–305

Objectives 1. To identify verbs as either action verbs or linking verbs

2. To differentiate between transitive and intransitive verbs

Presenting the Lesson 1. Read page 303. Stress the definitions of action verbs and linking verbs. Use the examples at the bottom of page 303 to illustrate how one verb can be used either as an action verb or as a linking verb.

2. Read page 304. Stress that the words *transitive* and *intransitive* only apply to action verbs. To help students understand the concept of *transitive* and *intransitive,* you may want to ask if they know what *transit* means. Explain that *transitive* is derived from the Latin word meaning "to pass over to." A transitive verb passes its action over to a stated direct object. An intransitive verb's action is complete in itself, rather than passed on to a direct object. Remind students that *in-* is a negative prefix, making *intransitive* mean "not carrying its action over to an object."

3. Assign and discuss Exercise A on page 304. For additional prac-

tice, have students tell whether each action verb is transitive or intransitive.

4. Assign and discuss Exercise B on page 305. For all transitive verbs, have students identify the direct object.

Optional Practice Have students identify the verb in each of the following sentences. Students should label each verb as *Action* or *Linking*. For each action verb, students should indicate whether the verb is transitive or intransitive.

1. Canvas covered the playing field.
2. Holidays seem more festive in small towns.
3. Six books fell from the shelf.
4. My winter parka feels so warm!
5. Janet looked ill this morning.
6. Hector can write with either hand.
7. Penny Marshall signed her name on the picture.
8. The United States sells much grain to foreign countries.
9. This book has been very interesting so far.
10. The warning lights flashed.

Extending the Lesson Have students write sentences using the following verbs in the ways indicated.

1. taste (action—transitive)
2. taste (linking)
3. run (action—intransitive)
4. sound (action—transitive)
5. sound (linking)

Part 2 **Helping Verbs and Main Verbs**   pp. 305–307

Objective To identify main verbs, helping verbs, and separated verb parts

Presenting the Lesson 1. Read pages 305 and 306. Go over the list of commonly used helping verbs. Emphasize that some verbs may be used either as helping verbs or as main verbs.

2. Assign and discuss Exercises A and B. Be certain that students have identified all separated verb parts in numbers 4 and 10.

Optional Practice   Have students identify the main verbs and the helping verbs in these sentences.

1. Is everyone going to the pep rally?
2. Someone is knocking on our back door.
3. Can you imagine such a surprise?
4. Your briefcase is open.
5. Lisa is opening her gifts now.
6. The plant should be turned toward the sun.
7. The room should never be too warm.
8. Snow was already falling this afternoon.
9. The book has a blue and green cover.
10. Josh has been working hard this year.

Extending the Lesson   Have students write sentences using the following verbs as indicated.

1. *crying* plus two helping verbs
2. *might have been* plus a main verb
3. *was* as a main verb
4. *was* as a helping verb
5. *could be* plus a main verb
6. *could* plus a main verb in a question
7. *been* plus a helping verb
8. *should be* plus a main verb
9. *enjoyed* plus a helping verb
10. *did* plus a main verb in a question

Part 3   **The Tenses of Verbs**   pp. 307–309

Objectives   1. To understand the concept of verb tense
2. To use verbs in the simple tenses and the perfect tenses

Presenting the Lesson   1. Read pages 307 and 308. Go over definitions of *tense, present tense, past tense,* and *future tense.* Use the following structure to help students see the changes in meaning and form. Write the headings *Today, Yesterday,* and *Tomorrow* on the board.

Ask students to fill in sentences using the appropriate forms of these verbs: *work, eat, go, jump,* and *clean.* Students should note the addition of *-ed* and the changes in spelling to form the past tense, and the use of *shall* or *will* with present tense to form the future tense.

2. Read the bottom of page 308. Explain that the three perfect tenses are used to compare actions occurring at two times.

The present perfect tense is used to refer to some indefinite time in the past or to show action that began in the past and continues into the present. For example:

> Eric has already begun his homework.
> Julie has studied piano for eight years.

The past perfect tense tells of an action completed in the past before some other past action. For example:

> Mike had never seen a skyscraper before he visited New York.

The future perfect tense tells of an action that will be completed before some other time in the future. For example:

> By the time we arrive in Seattle, we will have travelled
> through five towns.

Have students form the perfect tenses of these verbs: *talk, paint, close, live,* and *write.*

3. Assign and discuss Exercise A on page 309.

4. Assign and discuss Exercise B on page 309.

Optional Practice   Have students identify the verbs in each sentence and name their tenses.

1. What was your motive?

2. Dan will have finished painting the shelves by tonight.

3. Shall I leave with you?

4. His car has run out of gas.

5. Their family goes to church every week.

6. That librarian always sends me back to class.

7. Mary folded her paycheck carefully.

8. Have you recorded your answers?

9. I will never eat in this diner again.

10. We had laughed ourselves to tears by the time the intermission began.

Part 4

The Principal Parts of Verbs

Objective   To identify and form the principal parts of regular verbs

Presenting the Lesson   1. Read pages 309 and 310. Explain that the verbs dealt with in this part are called regular verbs because the past and the past participle are the same and are formed by adding -d or -ed to the present. Students must be reminded that spelling changes such as in *try—tried* or *knit—knitted* do not affect the status of a verb as a regular verb.

2. Assign and discuss the exercise on page 310.

Optional Practice   Have students list principal parts of these verbs.

plan	kill
scrub	play
slap	marry
blend	place
mix	scream

Extending the Lesson   Have students write sentences using each of the principal parts of five of the verbs in the exercise on page 310.

Part 5

Irregular Verbs

Objective   To use the principal parts of irregular verbs correctly

Presenting the Lesson   1. Review with students what is meant by principal parts of verbs. Ask students to recall why the verbs dealt with in Part 4 were called regular verbs. Stress that those verbs are regular because their past and past participle are the same. Both parts are formed by adding -d or -ed to the present.

Ask students if it is acceptable English to say "I eat, I eated, I have eated" or "he thinks, he thinked, he had thinked." Explain that many commonly used verbs are irregular in the way their past and past participle are formed.

2. Read pages 310 and 311. Go over the dictionary entry on page 311.

3. Read page 312 and the top of page 313. Read aloud the principal parts of all verbs listed. For added practice, have students use principal parts from the list of irregular verbs in sentences.

4. Assign and discuss Exercises A and B on page 313. Have students tell whether the correct form is the past or the past participle.

5. Read page 314, again reading principal parts aloud, and again having students use various parts in sentences.

6. Assign and discuss Exercises A and B on pages 314–315.

7. Read page 315, following the same procedure with verbs in Group 4 as done for previous groups.

8. Assign and discuss Exercises A and B on pages 315 and 316.

9. Read pages 316 and 317, handling verbs in Group 5 as done with previous groups.

10. Assign and discuss Exercises A and B on page 317.

Optional Practice   Have students fill the blank in each of the following sentences with the correct form of the verb in parentheses. Students should tell whether the form used is the past or the past participle.

1. I should have (know) _____ better.

2. Have the lawyers (choose) _____ the jury members?

3. The alarm (ring) _____ to warn the guards.

4. The Beatles (begin) _____ to be famous in 1963.

5. The thieves were (catch) _____ making their getaway.

6. Our neighbor has (lend) _____ us his lawnmower.

7. The knees on my jeans (wear) _____ out, so I put patches on them.

8. Who could have (drink) _____ all the milk?

9. The poem was (write) _____ especially for you.

10. Leaves (fall) _____ from the wind-blown trees.

Part 6   **Troublesome Pairs of Verbs**   pp. 318–321

Objective   To use the principal parts of troublesome pairs of verbs correctly: *learn* and *teach, let* and *leave, lie* and *lay, may* and *can, rise* and *raise, sit* and *set*

Presenting the Lesson   1. Read and discuss pages 318–320. Stress the difference in meaning and use between the verbs in each pair.

2. Assign and discuss Exercises A and B on page 321. In going over items, have students state why each sentence requires the one correct verb. Have students tell the meaning of the verb used.

Optional Practice   Have students write the indicated forms of each of the following verbs and then use each in a sentence.

1. past participle of *sit*
2. present of *raise*
3. past of *raise*
4. past participle of *rise*
5. past of *set*
6. past of *lie*
7. past of *lay*
8. past participle of *lie*
9. past of *let*
10. past of *teach*
11. past participle of *learn*

Review

pp. 322–323

You may use the review on pages 322–323 either as a checkup or for additional practice.

HANDBOOK SECTION 6

Using Modifiers

Pages 324–346

Objectives

1. To recognize adjectives and understand their function
2. To form and use the comparative and superlative forms of adjectives correctly
3. To recognize adverbs and understand their function in modifying verbs, adjectives, or other adverbs
4. To form and use the comparative and superlative forms of adverbs correctly
5. To differentiate between adverbs and adjectives and to use the correct modifier in sentences
6. To avoid special problems with modifiers: *them* and *those*, the extra *here* and *there*, *kind* and *sort*, *good* and *well*, and the double negative

Preparing the Students

Explain to students that while a sentence may be complete when it consists of a subject and verb (*The swimmer dived.*), it will be much more vivid and specific if modifiers are used to describe it. (The inexperienced swimmer dived awkwardly. The terrified swimmer dived recklessly. The professional swimmer dived faultlessly.) Modifiers—adjectives and adverbs—are necessary for adding detail and precision to writing.

Read the introduction on page 324 with the students.

Part 1 **Adjectives**   pp. 325–328

Objective   To recognize adjectives and understand their function

Presenting the Lesson   1. Read page 325. Make certain that students understand the meaning of *modify* and the definition of *adjective*. Study the examples of how adjectives function in three ways. Using the following additional examples, ask students to identify the adjectives and say whether they tell *what kind, how many,* or *which one*.

> Good things come in small packages.
> The security guard will search these bags.
> Alice spilled three cups of steaming coffee.
> This weather reminds me of our splendid vacation in
>   sunny Florida.

2. Read the bottom of page 325. Remind students that while the proper adjective is capitalized, the noun that it modifies is not capitalized.

3. Read page 326 dealing with predicate adjectives and articles.

4. Read pages 326 and 327 dealing with diagramming adjectives. Study examples showing the placement of adjectives, articles, predicate adjectives, and compound predicate adjectives.

5. Assign and discuss Exercise A on pages 327–328. In going over the exercise, have students explain what each adjective tells about the noun or pronoun it modifies.

6. Assign and discuss Exercise B on page 328.

Extending the Lesson   Have students diagram the following sentences.

1. That tall pine tree looks perfect.
2. A noisy, enthusiastic crowd met the popular Japanese baseball team.
3. Kevin wore a navy wool suit.
4. The British film was interesting and funny.
5. This new travel guide is informative and colorful.

Part 2 **Adjectives in Comparisons** pp. 328–331

Objective   To form and use the comparative and superlative forms of adjectives correctly

Presenting the Lesson   1. Read pages 328–330. Go over the rules for using comparatives on page 330. Read the list of irregular comparisons on page 330.
2. Assign and discuss Exercise A and B on page 331. In correcting errors, have students tell why the correction is necessary.

Optional Practice   Have students list the comparative and superlative forms of the following adjectives and then write sentences using each comparative and superlative form.

1. hot	5. enjoyable	9. delightful
2. noisy	6. eager	10. much
3. clean	7. crazy	
4. cautious	8. bad	

Part 3 **Adverbs** pp. 331–335

Objective   To recognize adverbs and understand their function in modifying verbs, adjectives, or other adverbs

Presenting the Lesson   1. Read pages 331 and 332. Stress the four ways in which adverbs modify verbs. Study the examples of adverbs which fit into each category. Have students add adverbs to the following sentence as they were added to the example: *The quarterback threw the ball.* Students should add several different adverbs to tell *how, when, where,* and *to what extent.*

2. Read pages 332–333 regarding use of adverbs with adjectives or other adverbs. Have students add several different adverbs to modify the adjective or adverb in these sentences: *Jan walked slowly. The baby was fussy.*

3. Read pages 333 and 334 dealing with the formation of adverbs. Tell students that in order to determine whether a word such as *early* or *fast* is an adjective or adverb, they should decide what word it modifies. If it modifies a noun or pronoun, it is an adjective. If it modifies a verb, adjective or adverb, it is an adverb.

4. Read page 334 on diagramming adverbs. Go over examples.

5. Assign and discuss Exercises A and B on pages 334–335.

6. Assign and discuss Exercise C on page 335.

Optional Practice   Have students supply adverbs to fill in blanks in the following sentences.

1. The time passed _____ during the exam.

2. Bob _____ forgets to wash the dishes.

3. Gretchen laughed _____ at the joke.

4. The team rowed the boat _____.

5. Some _____ spicy pizza made my stomach feel jumpy.

6. The bus travelled _____ along the highway.

7. Joel's handwriting is _____ impossible to read.

8. Come _____ to help with the project.

9. The bells chimed _____ and _____.

10. We searched _____ for something to eat.

Part 4   **Adverbs in Comparisons**   pp. 335–338

Objective   To form and use the comparative and superlative forms of adverbs correctly

Presenting the Lesson   1. Remind students of the major points studied regarding adjectives in comparisons. Review the use of comparative adjectives to compare two things, and superlative adjectives to compare more than two things. Review also the formation of comparative and superlative by the addition of *-er, -est,* or *more* and *most.*

2. Read pages 335–337. Go over the four rules to keep in mind for using adverbs in comparisons. Go over examples of adverbs

which have complete word changes to form their comparatives and superlatives.

3. Assign and discuss Exercises A and B on page 338.

Optional Practice   Have students write the comparative and superlative forms of each of the following adverbs and use each comparative and superlative form in a sentence.

1. easily   6. well
2. eagerly   7. hurriedly
3. long   8. wisely
4. carefully   9. early
5. seriously   10. quickly

Extending the Lesson   Have students supply comparative or superlative adverbs to complete the following sentences.

1. The young pitcher threw _____ than the pitching coach.
2. Linda did her work _____ than her sister.
3. Of all the animals in the game preserve, the jaguar moves _____ .
4. Lauren seems to skate the _____ of all the members on the hockey team.
5. This typewriter works _____ than that one.

Part 5 **Adjective or Adverb?**   pp. 338–341

Objective   To differentiate between adverbs and adjectives and to use the correct modifier in sentences

Presenting the Lesson   1. Read page 338. Go over the distinctions between adjectives and adverbs, stressing what each modifier tells about the word it modifies.

2. Do Exercise A together with the class. As each modifier is identified, have students tell whether it is an adverb or an adjective. Besides telling what word it modifies, students should tell the part of speech of the word modified, and what the modifier tells about the word modified. Refer to the chart on page 338.

3. Assign and discuss Exercise B on page 339.

4. Read page 340 regarding adverbs and predicate adjectives. Remind students that when a predicate adjective follows a linking verb, it describes the subject. When an adverb follows an action verb, it describes the action of the verb.

5. Assign and discuss the exercise on page 341. In addition to choosing the right modifier, have students tell whether the modifier is an adverb or an adjective. Students should double check their choices by identifying the sentence's verb as action or linking.

Optional Practice   Have students identify modifiers in the following sentences and tell whether each is an adjective or adverb.

1. The unhappy children complained bitterly.
2. Our long hike in the national park was enjoyable.
3. Roberta spread peanut butter and jelly thickly on the fresh bread.
4. The spectators shouted angrily, and the players became furious.
5. Richie and the Fonz always handle their problems cheerfully, but real situations are more complex.

Part 6   **Special Problems with Modifiers**   pp. 341–344

Objective   To avoid special problems with modifiers: *them* and *those*, the extra *here* and *there*, *kind* and *sort*, *good* and *well*, and the double negative

Presenting the Lesson   1. Read pages 341–343 and discuss each possible problem situation. Stress the examples and their explanations.

2. Assign and discuss Exercise A on pages 343–344. Ask students why the correct choice is needed.

3. Assign and discuss Exercise B on page 344. Ask students to tell whether the correct modifier is an adjective or an adverb, and to tell why that particular part of speech is needed.

4. Assign and discuss Exercise C on page 344.

Optional Practice   Have students correct errors in the following sentences. If the sentence has no errors, it should be labeled *Correct*. Students should be able to explain why the correction is needed.

1. Does that there hamburger look rightly to you?
2. Everyone likes them jogging shoes.

3. Those kind of doughnuts become stale quick.

4. Nancy looks good, but she doesn't feel good.

5. John Travolta isn't no good in his most recent movie.

6. Things don't ever go as well for me as for that there senior.

7. This sort of equipment protects you as well as that kind.

8. We haven't hardly begun to practice good.

9. Doesn't that there boy feel well?

10. What kind of sun tan cream works well for you?

Review

pp. 345–346

You may use the review on pages 345 and 346 ether as a check-up or for additional practice.

Using Prepositions and Conjunctions

Pages 347–359

Objectives

1. To recognize prepositions and prepositional phrases and to understand their functions

2. To distinguish between prepositions and adverbs

3. To determine whether a prepositional phrase functions as an adjective phrase or an adverb phrase

4. To recognize coordinating and correlative conjunctions and to understand their functions

Preparing the Students

Ask students if they can think of a smoother, more efficient way to state the following information:

It was the Fourth of July weekend. It was very hot. I had a picnic. My family had a picnic. The city park is where we had the picnic. There is a lake there. It has ducks. There are trees. There are flowers. There are picnic tables. There is space to play softball. We enjoyed our afternoon together. We want to go again soon.

The following is a suggested revision:

It was the Fourth of July weekend *and* it was very hot. My family *and* I had a picnic *in* the city park. There is a lake *in* the park *with* ducks *on* it. There are trees, flowers, picnic tables, *and* space to play softball *in* the park. We enjoyed our afternoon together, *and* we want to go again soon.

Point out the italicized words in the preceding paragraph and have the students note how these words are used to connect ideas.

Part 1 **Prepositions**   pp. 348–351

Objectives 1. To recognize prepositions and prepositional phrases and to understand their function

2. To distinguish between prepositions and adverbs

Presenting the Lesson 1. Read page 348. Stress that prepositions are connectives; they serve to connect a noun or pronoun to another part of the sentence. If students look at the word *preposition*, they should see in it the word *position*. Prepositions tell the position of their objects in terms of time, location, or other special relationships.

2. Go over the list of words often used as prepositions on page 349. Go around the classroom and have students use each preposition in a sentence. Have students describe the relationship indicated by the preposition.

3. Assign and discuss Exercises A and B on pages 349 and 350.

4. Read *Preposition or Adverb?* on page 350. Remind students that both prepositions and adverbs can tell *where* or *when* or *how*, but that prepositions always occur in phrases rather than by themselves.

5. Assign and discuss Exercises A and B on pages 350 and 351.

Optional Practice Have students identify prepositional phrases in the following sentences.

1. After the game the team rushed to the locker room.

2. The ink in my pen ran dry over the weekend.

3. The car turned down this street and into the alley.

4. Gwen told us about the trip she took with her family to Nashville.

5. Between the stream and the forest, we pitched our tents in a circle around the campfire.

Extending the Lesson Have students complete each of the following sentences in three different ways using three different prepositional phrases.

1. The nuclear energy plant is located _____

2. The airplane flew _____

3. Our city needs improvement _____

4. Everyone _____ feels better when the sun shines.

5. The animals can be kept _____

Part 2 **Prepositional Phrases as Modifiers** pp. 351–354

Objective To determine whether a prepositional phrase functions as an adjective phrase or an adverb phrase

Presenting the Lesson 1. Read pages 351–353. Study examples carefully, noting explanations telling what each phrase tells about the word it modifies. Pay special attention to examples of two successive prepositional phrases.
2. Study diagrams of prepositional phrases on page 353.
3. Assign and discuss Exercises A and B on page 354.

Extending the Lesson Have students write the following sentences, placing the prepositional phrases in the correct places.

1. Jack was looking for a notebook. (at the stationery store) (without lines)

2. Chris has been studying piano. (with the same teacher) (for three years)

3. The sailboat glided out. (with four passengers) (of the harbor)

4. There was a family of cats. (under the porch) (with long hair)

5. One team will meet. (in the park) (after dinner) (for basketball practice)

6. There was a horse. (on the other side) (with a long silky tail)

7. We planted a garden. (with flower and vegetable seeds) (between the house and the driveway)

8. I ran. (after school) (to Terry's house) (through the open field)

9. Judy painted the bookcase. (in the backyard) (before lunch) (with white paint)

10. Ted and I hurried. (at five o'clock) (of the hospital volunteer group) (to the meeting)

Part 3 **Conjunctions**   pp. 355–357

Objective To recognize coordinating and correlative conjunctions and to understand their functions

Presenting the Lesson 1. Read the top of page 355, emphasizing the definition of *conjunction* and the examples of sentences containing conjunctions.

2. Analyze the word *conjunction* with students to help them understand what conjunctions are. Ask students to tell you what a *junction* is. They will no doubt relate the word to the coming together of two streets or roads. Explain that a junction is a point of joining. The word part *con* means *with*. Thus, a conjunction serves to join two words or groups of words with one another.

3. Read pages 355 and 356, explaining coordinating conjunctions. Go over examples carefully, making certain students understand which sentence parts are made compound by the use of conjunctions.

4. Read page 356 about correlative conjunctions.

5. Assign and discuss Exercises A, B, and C on pages 356–357.

Optional Practice Assign the following exercise: Have students write the kind of compound constructions they find in each of the following sentences. Students should write the constructions with their conjunctions.

1. Both the lights and the telephones were cut off by the hail storm.

2. Please turn off the radio and the record player.

3. The wind blew our garbage cans and patio furniture into the street.

4. The weight lifter strained and struggled as he lifted the heaviest weights.

5. I tried but couldn't open the jar of peanut butter.

6. My favorite movies were *Star Wars* and *The Empire Strikes Back*.

7. Did the detective find any clues or fingerprints?

8. Neither Mary nor Glenda was on time for the bus.

9. The picnic will be held whether it is warm or not.

10. Gabriel felt ill but went to class anyway.

Review

pp. 358–359

You may use the Review on pages 358–359 either as a checkup or for additional practice.

Review of Parts of Speech
Pages 360–364

Objectives

1. To recognize and use interjections
2. To review the eight parts of speech
3. To recognize the use of a single word as different parts of speech

Preparing the Students

Ask students to name the seven parts of speech studied thus far. Ask for several examples of each part of speech. Ask students why each part of speech is important in helping to communicate. Explain that Section 8 will present a review of the seven parts of speech, and it will also present the eighth part of speech.

Objectives 1. To recognize and use interjections

2. To review the eight parts of speech

Presenting the Lesson 1. Read pages 360 and 361. Ask students to suggest more words or phrases commonly used as interjections.

2. Review the eight parts of speech listed in the box on page 361. Review definitions, functions, and examples of each part of speech.

3. Do Exercise A on page 361 orally with the class. As students identify parts of speech, have them tell how they function in each sentence.

4. Assign and discuss Exercise B on pages 361 and 362.

Extending the Lesson Have students identify the parts of speech of each word in the following sentences. Students should be prepared to tell how each part of speech functions in the sentence.

1. Your new brown purse is beautiful.

2. Can Seymour play first base?

3. Heavens! The leaves are falling from the trees already.

4. Neither breakfast nor lunch appealed to me.

5. We traveled to Boston by bus.

Part 2 **Words Used as Different Parts of Speech**
pp. 362–363

Objective To recognize the use of a single word as various parts of speech

Presenting the Lesson 1. Read pages 362 and 363, studying examples of words used as two different parts of speech. Remind students that they have already studied some words that may be used as two different parts of speech: pronouns and adjectives (page 300), prepositions and adverbs (page 350), adjectives and adverbs (page 338).

2. Assign and discuss Exercises A and B on page 363.

Optional Practice Have students identify the part of speech of the italicized word or words in each sentence.

1. *Close* the door.

2. *Boy!* was that a *close call.*

3. That *boy* should *call* his father.

4. The magician will *place* the card *under* the pile.

5. Our puppy found a *place* on the fence where he could crawl *under.*

6. *These flies* are driving me crazy.

7. *These* are the jets Delta *flies* to Miami.

8. After you *lock* the car, come *over* to the office.

9. Jon put a *lock on* his locker.

10. The dog rolled *over.*

Extending the Lesson   Have students look up the following words in the dictionary and list all possible parts of speech for each. Students should write original sentences using each word as the parts of speech listed.

1. run   2. pass   3. thin   4. score   5. slide

HANDBOOK SECTION 9

Sentence Patterns

Pages 365–372

Objectives

1. To understand how word order affects meaning
2. To recognize the NV sentence pattern
3. To recognize the NVN sentence pattern
4. To recognize the NVNN sentence pattern
5. To recognize the N LV N sentence pattern
6. To recognize the N LV Adj sentence pattern

Preparing the Students

Play this game with students to impress upon them the importance of word order and the patterns into which words are placed to express meaning. Divide the class into four groups, two groups of five students and two groups of seven.

Give each group a pack of index cards which you have prepared ahead of time. One word should be written on each card. Packs should contain these words.

Pack 1	Pack 2
mechanic	ice cream
the	sister
fixed	strawberry
our	likes
car	my

Pack 3	Pack 4
boy	father
elderly	my
woman	my
a	gift
seat	brought
gave	a
the	sister
his	birthday

Students in each group should take one card each. By studying the entire group's cards and by discussing how the words can be arranged, students should attempt to make a meaningful sentence out of the words. Groups can line up in order of a meaningful sentence, showing their cards to the class.

The rest of the class should try to see similarities between word order in groups 1 and 2 and groups 3 and 4. To help students see similarity, you can do the following while groups are lined up in front of the class. Have "noun" students step forward and "verb" students step back. Class should see that nouns and verbs take similar positions in groups 1 and 2, and groups 3 and 4.

Read the introduction on page 365.

Part 1 **Word Order and Meaning** p. 366

Objective   To understand how word order affects meaning

Presenting the Lesson   1. Read page 366. Explain that altering word order of a sentence may make the sentence mean something different or may make it meaningless.

2. Assign the Exercise on page 366.

Optional Practice   Have students put the following group of words in meaningful order. Have them put an asterisk (*) before sentences which could be meaningful in a different order.

1. a Vincent bowl Cheerios of ate
2. outside raining today is it
3. prescribed cold my for the doctor medicine
4. movie cartoon showed a before they the
5. Ed a member is of band school the

Part 2   **The N V Pattern**   p. 364

Objective   To recognize the NV sentence pattern

Presenting the Lesson   1. Read page 367 and study the examples of the NV pattern. Explain that the pattern of NV is not altered by the addition of modifiers (adjectives, adverbs, prepositional phrases) or articles. Explain that even a compound subject or verb can be included in a NV pattern. Present these additional examples, all in the NV pattern.

N   V
Spiderman arrived.

N   V
Caroline called.

N   V
The villain escaped.

N   V
Dark clouds moved in.

N   V
Girls and boys played on the swings.

2. Assign and discuss Exercises A, B, and C on page 364.

Optional Practice   Have students place N and V over the appropriate words in the following NV sentences.

1. My gold shirt ripped during the dance practice.
2. The exhausted fireman collapsed.
3. The tires of the jeep spun in the mud.
4. A cold draft blew on us.
5. Ruth missed the bus this morning.

Objective   To recognize the NVN sentence pattern

Presenting the Lesson   Read page 368 and study the examples of the NVN pattern. Remind students that the V in this pattern will always be a transitive action verb. Again stress that modifiers can be added to sentences without affecting the NVN pattern. Use the two examples below and point out that both are in the NVN pattern. Have students identify the N, V and N in each.

> We watched television.
> None of us at home ever watches television early in the morning.

Optional Practice   Have students create NVN sentences using the words below in the designated positions.

1. predicted   (verb)
2. reporter   (subject)
3. visited   (verb)
4. ice cream   (direct object)
5. government   (subject)

Objective   To recognize the NVNN sentence pattern

Presenting the Lesson   1. Read page 369 and study the examples of the NVNN pattern.
2. Assign and discuss Exercises A, B, and C on page 369.

Optional Practice   Have students mark N, V, N, and N over the subject, verb, indirect object, and direct object in these sentences.

1. My aunt's rose garden gives me an asthma attack.
2. Mr. Drummond read us the newspaper article.
3. You can send your boss a bill for your transportation.
4. Snoopy brings Woodstock his birdseed.
5. Nancy is knitting Jerry a scarf.

Extending the Lesson   Explain to students that the three patterns dealt with thus far (NV, NVN, NVNN) have all contained action verbs. Explain that in the NV pattern, the action verb is intransitive; it has no object. In the NVN and the NVNN pattern, the action verb is transitive; it has a direct object. Have students make up sentences using the verbs as indicated. Students may add helping verbs. For each sentence created, students should write the pattern.

1. offered (transitive)
2. runs (intransitive)
3. shake (transitive)
4. tell (transitive)
5. rained (intransitive)

Have students use each verb below in a NVN and a NVNN sentence.

1. bring   2. sell   3. write

Part 5   **The N LV N Pattern**   p. 370

Objective   To recognize the N LV N sentence pattern

Presenting the Lesson   1. Read page 370, studying examples of the N LV N pattern. Remind students that a pronoun may be substituted for either noun in the pattern. Stress that this type of sentence differs from the N V N sentence in that the N LV N sentence contains a linking verb rather than an action verb. In the N LV N pattern, there is a link or equality between the two nouns. The predicate noun renames the subject. The nouns in a N LV N sentence can be reversed without a change in meaning.

> Elton John is my favorite singer.
> My favorite singer is Elton John.

2. Assign and discuss Exercises A, B, and C on page 370.

Optional Practice   Have students create N LV N sentences using the following nouns in the position indicated.

1. Julie   (subject)
2. Colorado   (predicate noun)
3. lawyer   (predicate noun)
4. Mayor Byrne   (subject)
5. whale   (predicate noun)

Part 6

The N LV Adj Pattern

Objective To recognize the N LV Adj sentence pattern

Presenting the Lesson 1. Read page 371. Study the examples of N LV Adj sentences. Point out that while the N LV Adj sentence is similar to the N LV N in its use of a linking verb, the difference is in the use of a predicate adjective to describe the subject. Call students' attention to the use of a variety of state of being verbs (*looks, seems, tastes*) in the N LV Adj pattern. Review with students the differences between nouns and adjectives. Refer to pages 325 and 326.

2. Assign and discuss Exercises A, B, and C on page 371.

Optional Practice Have students label each of the following sentences as N LV N or N LV Adj.

1. De Paul University was the winner of today's game.

2. Their basketball team is undefeated.

3. The coach of the team is Ray Meyer.

4. He seems very devoted to his job as coach.

5. Basketball has always been my favorite sport.

Extending the Lesson Have students determine the pattern of each sentence below. Students should label sentences NV, NVN, NVNN, N LV N or N LV Adj.

1. Many states have ratified the Equal Rights Amendment.

2. Carnations always smell so fresh!

3. Jim Fixx has written several books about running.

4. Julia Child is a superb cook.

5. Mrs. Goldberg gave us a math test this morning.

6. Everyone cheered for the candidate.

7. Andy graduated in 1979.

8. Sarah looks different with her contact lenses.

9. My little brother became a Cub Scout this year.

10. A vet must give the dogs their shots.

Review

You may use the Review on page 372 either as a checkup or for additional practice.

Using Verbals

Objectives

1. To recognize gerunds and gerund phrases, and to understand the ways in which they are formed and used
2. To recognize participles and participial phrases, and to understand the ways in which they are formed and used
3. To distinguish between gerunds and participles
4. To recognize infinitives and infinitive phrases and to understand the ways in which they are formed and used
5. To avoid split infinitives
6. To review the formation and use of gerunds, participles, and infinitives

Preparing the Students

Read the introduction on page 373. Reassure students that while the names of the three types of verbals may sound difficult, students use verbals daily in their speaking and writing. Tell students that if they understand the following sentence, containing all three types of verbals, they can understand Section 10.

> To understand verbals requires studying common spoken and written constructions.

Part 1 **Gerunds**

pp. 374–377

Objective   To recognize gerunds and gerund phrases, and to understand the ways in which they are formed and used

Presenting the Lesson   1. Read page 374 defining a gerund. Point out that gerunds are always the *-ing* form of a verb. Study the examples showing gerunds in typical uses. Remind students that a gerund may be used as a predicate noun too. For example: Barbara's hobby is collecting stamps.

2. Read pages 374 and 375 presenting gerund phrases. Go over ex-

amples carefully. Students may find it confusing that gerunds can be modified by both adverbs and adjectives. Stress that gerunds come from verbs and are used as nouns.

3. Read pages 375 and 376 showing how to diagram gerunds and gerund phrases. Study sample diagrams which show the special nature of these words.

4. Assign and discuss Exercises A and B on pages 376 and 377. Students should notice how frequently gerunds are used as subjects of sentences.

Extending the Lesson Have students create sentences using the following gerunds or gerund phrases in the positions indicated.

1. eating too much (object of preposition)
2. voting for class officers (subject)
3. playing my guitar (direct object)
4. tumbling and vaulting (direct object)
5. landing the aircraft smoothly (subject)

Part 2 **Participles**   pp. 377–380

Objectives 1. To recognize participles and participial phrases, and to understand the ways in which they are formed and used

2. To distinguish between gerunds and participles

Presenting the Lesson 1. Read page 377 defining participles. Some review of past participles might be beneficial. Look at pages 309–320, paying particular attention to past participle forms of irregular verbs. Explain to students that when used as a verbal, a participle has no helping verbs and functions as an adjective. Ask students to supply the past participle form for the following irregular verbs: *feel, throw, cost, lead, freeze, begin.* Note that all present participles are formed by adding *-ing* to the present tense. Then have students form the present participle for these verbs: *do, grow.*

2. Go over the examples of how participles are used on the bottom of page 377.

3. Read page 378 discussing participial phrases. As with gerunds, stress that participles are verb forms used as another part of speech (adjectives). Thus, they can exhibit properties of verbs (have direct objects, be modified by adverbs, etc.) while they function as adjectives (modifying nouns or pronouns).

4. Read pages 378 and 379 showing how to diagram participles and participial phrases. Study the sample diagrams which help to indicate the special nature of participles.

5. Assign and discuss Exercises A and B on pages 379 and 380. Students should note the position of participial phrases in sentences in which the participial phrase modifies the subject.

6. Read page 380 which should help students distinguish between gerunds and participles. Point out that when a participle or a participial phrase begins a sentence (as a modifier of the subject), it is followed by a comma. A gerund or gerund phrase which begins a sentence (as the subject) is never followed by a comma.

7. Do the exercise on page 380 orally. Have students tell how the gerund or participle is used (as the subject, as a modifier of the subject, etc.).

Extending the Lesson Have students write sentences using the gerunds or participles in the manner indicated.

1. intercepting the pass (participle modifying subject)

2. broken (participle modifying subject)

3. losing his patience (participle modifying subject)

4. brushing your teeth (gerund as subject)

5. drinking soft drinks (gerund as direct object)

Part 3 **Infinitives** pp. 381–385

Objectives 1. To recognize infinitives and infinitive phrases and to understand the ways in which they are formed and used

2. To avoid split infinitives

Presenting the Lesson 1. Read pages 381–382 defining infinitives and infinitive phrases. Make certain that students understand the difference between the sign of the infinitive *to* and the preposition *to*. Have students identify the infinitives in the following sentences.

1. Mark said to follow him to school.

2. To educate yourself you must learn to ask questions.

3. I hope to go to your graduation.

4. Plan to arrive early; come to the back door.

5. Joan has gone to bed already because she wants to sleep ten hours tonight.

143

Go over the examples showing infinitives with objects and infinitives modified by adverbs and prepositional phrases.

2. Read pages 382 and 383 concerning uses of the infinitive phrase. Again stress to students that an infinitive is classified as a verbal because it is formed from a verb but used as another part of speech. Go over all examples of infinitives used as nouns, adjectives, and adverbs.

3. Read page 383 and discuss avoiding the split infinitive.

4. Read pages 383 and 384 showing how to diagram infinitives and infinitive phrases. Study the sample diagrams of infinitives which help to indicate the special nature of these words. Have students note how the infinitive can be used as a noun and as a modifier.

5. Assign and discuss Exercise A on page 384. In going over items, have students tell whether the infinitive functions as a noun, an adjective, or an adverb.

6. Assign and discuss Exercise B on page 384. Again, have students identify the function of each infinitive.

Extending the Lesson   Have students write sentences using the following infinitives and infinitive phrases in the ways indicated.

> 1. to win the gold medal (noun as direct object)
>
> 2. to earn extra money (adverb)
>
> 3. to grow vegetables (noun as direct object)
>
> 4. to play hockey (noun as subject)
>
> 5. to take photographs (adjective)

Part 4   **A Review of Verbals**   pp. 385–386

Objective   To review the formation and use of gerunds, participles, and infinitives

Presenting the Lesson   1. Read pages 385 and 386. Go over the definitions of verbals, gerunds, participles, and infinitives. Study the examples of the three types of verbals.

2. Do Exercise A on page 386 orally. Have students also tell how each verbal is used (as subject, adjective, etc.).

3. Assign and discuss Exercise B on page 386.

Optional Practice   Have students write sentences using the following verbals. For each sentence, students should tell whether the verbal is a gerund, participle, or infinitive and tell how it is used in the sentence.

1. zipping his jacket
2. to forget my lunch
3. going to college
4. frightened by the siren
5. jogging along the lake
6. to score a touchdown
7. reading novels
8. sliding into second base
9. to lose ten pounds
10. shaking her head

Review

p. 387

You may use the Review on page 387 either as a checkup or for additional practice.

Making Subjects and Verbs Agree
Pages 388–396

Objectives

1. To make verbs agree in number with their subjects
2. To use a verb that agrees in number with compound subjects
3. To use a verb that agrees in number with an indefinite pronoun that is its subject
4. To avoid errors in agreement between subjects and verbs in sentences using *don't* and *doesn't* and in sentences beginning with *here*, *there*, and *where*

Preparing the Students

Explain to students that sometimes while getting dressed you might glance in the mirror and say, "These pants just don't go with this shirt." In language, too, some combinations just don't agree with one another. Section 11 will help students match verbs and subjects which do agree. Read the introduction on page 388.

Part 1 **Making Subjects and Verbs Agree in Number**
pp. 388–390

Objective   To make verbs agree in number with their subjects

Presenting the Lesson   1. Read page 388 and the top of page 389. Make certain that students understand the meaning of *singular, plural,* and *number*. To be sure that students can distinguish between singular and plural subjects and verbs, write these verbs on the board: *walk, sit, drink, cry, laugh.* Have students supply an appropriate singular or plural form of one of the verbs to go with each of the following subjects. Ask students to tell whether these matched subjects and verbs are singular or plural.

1. birds
2. children
3. a baby
4. people

5. a woman
6. three men
7. we
8. she

9. David
10. the audience

2. Read the balance of page 389 dealing with ways to determine the subject when phrases are also present. Have students identify the subjects in the following sentences.

1. One of your shoelaces is untied.
2. My keys, as well as my wallet, are at home.
3. Gloria, together with Archie and Edith, is coming.
4. The geese in the pond need to be fed.
5. All of the books on the shelf are dusty.

3. Assign and discuss Exercises A and B on page 390. Have students identify each subject and tell whether it is singular or plural.

Optional Practice   Present the following sentences to students on a worksheet. Two of the sentences are correct while the others contain errors in agreement between subject and verb. For each sentence, have students identify the subject, tell whether it is singular or plural, and determine if the verb agrees in number. If the sentence is correct, have students write C. If the verb does not agree with the subject, have students correct the verb.

1. My sweater, together with a down vest, keep me warm.
2. The sheets of paper left on the pad is not enough.
3. The sentences in the exercise are easy.
4. Refills for my favorite pen keeps going up in price.
5. Crime, as well as poverty, are a problem in our city.
6. Each child, together with his or her parents, has a conference with the teacher.
7. One of the straps on my ski boots are broken.
8. The ladder, together with the scaffold, weigh over three hundred pounds.
9. A ticket, including door prizes, cost five dollars.
10. A house in the suburbs do not appeal to my family.

Part 2 **Compound Subjects**   pp. 391–392

Objective To use verbs that agree in number with compound subjects

Presenting the Lesson 1. Read page 391. Point out the difference between compound subjects joined by *and* (always requiring a plural verb) and those joined by *or* or *nor* (requiring a verb which agrees with the nearer subject).
2. Do Exercise A on page 391 orally with the class. Have students tell why the verb chosen is correct.
3. Assign and discuss Exercise B on pages 391 and 392.

Optional Practice Have students complete the following sentences using verbs that agree with the compound subjects given. Students should be prepared to tell why they have used a singular or plural verb.

1. The boss and her secretary _____.
2. The carpet and drapes _____.
3. Either the doctor or the nurses _____.

4. Neither my cousins nor my aunt _____.

5. Either your records or your radio _____.

6. The papers and pencils _____.

7. The girls in the class and their teacher _____.

8. Neither Joy nor her close friends _____.

9. Four chairs and a table _____.

10. Either sandwiches or a salad _____.

Part 3 **Indefinite Pronouns**   pp. 392–393

Objective To use a verb that agrees in number with an indefinite pronoun that is its subject

Presenting the Lesson 1. Read pages 392 and 393. Go over the list of pronouns that are always singular. Have students practice using each of these singular indefinite pronouns as the subject of a sentence. Do the same with the indefinite pronouns that are always plural. Carefully study examples on page 393 of indefinite pronouns which can be either singular or plural. Remind students that phrases that appear between the subject and verb do not affect the number of the verb.

2. Assign and discuss Exercises A and B on pages 393 and 394.

Optional Practice Have students complete the following sentences using verbs which agree in number with their subjects.

1. Each of your grandparents _____.

2. Several of these exercises _____.

3. Most of the marbles _____.

4. Most of the milk _____.

5. Many of the drivers _____.

6. Everything in the drawers _____.

7. All of my muscles _____.

8. Some of the thread _____.

9. Few of the speakers _____.

10. Each of the guests _____.

Part 4

Other Problems of Agreement

Objective   To avoid errors in agreement between subjects and verbs in sentences using *don't* and *doesn't* and in sentences beginning with *here, there,* and *where*

Presenting the Lesson   1. Read page 394. Study examples of the correct use of *don't* and *doesn't*. Study examples of sentences beginning with *here, where,* and *there*. Be sure students identify the subject in each example.

2. Assign and discuss Exercises A and B on pages 394 and 395.

Optional Practice   Present the following sentences to students on a worksheet. Two of the sentences are correct, while the others contain errors in agreement between subject and verb. If the sentence is correct, have students write *C*. If the verb does not agree with the subject, have students correct the verb.

1. Donald don't do his share of the work.

2. Where is the newspapers?

3. Here are all of them.

4. Someone don't have his uniform cleaned.

5. There is too many people for our car.

6. Doesn't the windows need washing?

7. Where is everybody?

8. Where does these footprints come from?

9. Doesn't your parents let you stay out late?

10. Here is a few problems.

Review

p. 396

You may use the Review on page 396 either as a checkup or for additional practice.

Using Compound and Complex Sentences

Objectives

1. To review the parts of the simple sentence
2. To recognize and form compound sentences and to differentiate between compound sentences and simple sentences with compound predicates
3. To recognize and form complex sentences
4. To recognize main clauses and subordinate clauses and to distinguish clauses from phrases
5. To recognize subordinating conjunctions and understand their function
6. To recognize adverb clauses and to understand how they are used in sentences
7. To recognize adjective clauses and to understand how they are used in sentences
8. To recognize relative pronouns and to understand their function in introducing clauses
9. To recognize noun clauses and understand how they are used in sentences
10. To be able to identify noun, adverb, and adjective subordinate clauses
11. To be able to recognize and correct subordinate clause sentence fragments
12. To review simple, compound, and complex sentences

Preparing the Students

Explain to students that good writing, like good cooking, good music, or even a good vacation, depends upon variety. If all written sentences were similarly patterned simple sentences, writing would be choppy and monotonous. Section 12 will study three types of sentences, each of which contributes to good, interesting writing.

Part 1 **Review of the Sentence** pp. 397–400

Objective To review the parts of the simple sentence

Presenting the Lesson 1. Read pages 397–399. Review definitions of *simple subject, simple predicate, subject, predicate,* and *compound.* Look carefully at examples of compound sentence parts. Make sure that students understand the definition of a simple sentence.

2. Assign Exercise A on page 399. For additional practice, students should underline the subject once and the verb twice.

3. Assign and discuss Exercise B on pages 399 and 400.

Optional Practice Have students write sentences containing the following parts.

1. compound subject

2. compound predicate

3. compound subject and compound predicate

4. compound direct object

5. compound subject and compound predicate words

Part 2 **The Compound Sentence** pp. 400–407

Objective To recognize and form compound sentences and to differentiate between compound sentences and simple sentences with compound predicates

Presenting the Lesson 1. Read pages 400 and 401. Be sure that students understand the definition of a compound sentence and the usefulness of compound sentences. Study the examples at the bottom of page 400 showing the use of the three coordinating conjunctions and the semicolon to join compound sentences.

2. Read page 401 showing the way to diagram a compound sentence. Point out the use of the dotted line with a step for the coordinating conjunction.

3. Do Exercises A and B on page 402 as a class activity. Volunteers may put their answers on the board. Ask students in which sentences the coordinating conjunction could be replaced with a semicolon.

4. Read pages 403 and 404. Stress that in a compound sentence there will be two stated subjects as well as two stated verbs.

5. Do Exercise A on page 404 as a class activity. In addition to determining whether the sentences are compound or simple with a compound predicate, have students tell what the subject and verb of each sentence are.

6. Assign and discuss Exercise B on pages 404 and 405.

7. Read pages 405 and 406 discussing how to punctuate compound sentences. Make sure students understand why a comma is used before the coordinating conjunction. Point out that a semicolon may replace a coordinating conjunction, but may not be used with a coordinating conjunction. Study examples carefully.

8. Assign and discuss Exercises A and B on pages 406 and 407.

Optional Practice Have students form five compound sentences from the following ten simple sentences by combining closely related ideas. Students should add conjunctions and punctuation as necessary.

1. Joanna broke her leg.

2. The movie begins at 8:00.

3. Did anyone call while I was out?

4. The doctor put a cast on and gave her crutches.

5. Were there any deliveries?

6. Fred worked last summer.

7. I have to work until 9:00.

8. Our family is sports-minded.

9. Mom doesn't know the first thing about football.

10. He used the money to buy a bicycle.

Part 3 **Complex Sentences** pp. 407–411

Objectives 1. To recognize and form complex sentences

2. To recognize main clauses and subordinate clauses and to distinguish clauses from phrases

3. To recognize subordinating conjunctions and understand their function

Presenting the Lesson 1. Read pages 407 and 408 defining a clause. Study examples of clauses, and stress that while a clause may be a complete sentence, it should be thought of as a group of words within a sentence.

2. Read the bottom of page 408, studying examples of phrases and clauses. Ask students to identify the following groups of words as either phrases or clauses.

in a big hurry	during the intermission
as I waited for the bus	since it was warm outside
before anyone arrived	

3. Read page 409 and the top of page 410. Study the examples of subordinate clauses. Be sure students understand the definitions of *subordinate* and *dependent*. Carefully study the list of words often used as subordinating conjunctions. Ask students to offer examples of sentences containing subordinate clauses introduced by subordinating conjunctions on the list. Go over the list of other words which often introduce subordinate clauses on the top of page 410. Again, have students offer examples of sentences using these words to introduce subordinate clauses.

4. Assign the exercise at the top of page 410. In going over the exercise, have one student read his subordinate clause and another student add a main clause to complete the thought.

5. Read the definition of a complex sentence on page 410.

6. Assign and discuss Exercises A and B on pages 410 and 411.

Optional Practice Have students identify the italicized group of words in each sentence as a phrase, a main clause, or a subordinate clause.

1. The quiet room *in the library* is always empty.

2. *Since I have so much homework,* I will go there.

3. *While I am studying,* please fix dinner.

4. *Let's eat early tonight,* because there is a good program on TV.

5. *If I finish all my work,* I can even watch the late movie.

Extending the Lesson Have students make complex sentences out of these pairs of related sentences.

1. This is the sculpture. The city is going to replace.

2. You cannot park here. You have a special permit.

3. The wind blows off the lake. The temperature drops.

4. Elsie took the lower bunk. She is afraid of heights.

5. Bob didn't wear his glasses. He can't see the screen.

Objective To recognize adverb clauses and to understand how they are used in sentences

Presenting the Lesson 1. Read pages 411 and 412. Go over the definition of an adverb clause, studying examples to differentiate an adverb clause from an adverb phrase.
2. Go over the diagram of a sentence containing an adverb clause.
3. Do Exercise A on pages 412 and 413 as a class activity. After students locate adverb clauses and identify their subjects and verbs, have them also tell what word the clause modifies and what the clause tells about the word. Students should also identify the subordinate conjunction.
4. Assign and discuss Exercise B on page 413.

Optional Practice Have students complete the following complex sentences by adding words to each to form an adverb clause. Have students tell what word their clause modifies and what the clause tells about that word.

1. Jana can attend the movie if _____.
2. Since _____, you will have to do fifty push-ups.
3. My baby sister cries as soon as _____.
4. If _____, keep trying.
5. The official dropped his penalty flag when _____.

Extending the Lesson Have students rewrite the following compound sentences as complex sentences, using the list of subordinating conjunctions on page 409. Have them change the underlined clause into a subordinate clause.

1. *Pablo Picasso died,* and his paintings are even more valuable.
2. *We were so hungry* and we stopped at McDonald's.
3. The janitor swept the floor and *we waited in the hall.*
4. *The car was going too fast* and it almost missed the turn.
5. *Our team played its best* but we did not win the tournament.

Objectives 1. To recognize adjective clauses and to understand how they are used in sentences

2. To recognize relative pronouns and to understand their function in introducing clauses

Presenting the Lesson 1. Read pages 413 and 414. Go over the definition of an adjective clause. Study the examples of adjective clauses on page 414 noting the word each adjective clause modifies and what the clause tells about that word.

2. Read pages 414 and 415 discussing relative pronouns. Make sure students understand the three functions listed. Study examples.

3. Study the diagrams of sentences containing adjective clauses. Have students note how the subordinate adjective clause is placed below the main clause and connected by a dotted line to the noun or pronoun it modifies.

4. Do Exercise A on page 416 as a class activity.

5. Assign and discuss Exercise B on pages 416 and 417.

Optional Practice Have students complete the following complex sentences by adding words to form adjective clauses.

1. This is the room where _____.

2. The people who _____ called my home today.

3. One reason that _____ was the awful weather.

4. Peter is the person to whom _____.

5. Senator Baker is the leader who _____.

Extending the Lesson Have students rewrite each pair of sentences as a complex sentence, using the underlined sentence as the subordinate clause.

1. Where is the pen? I just had it. (that)

2. The new coach gave us some excellent advice. He had played on a championship team. (who)

3. The trees on our street had beautiful flowers this spring. They were planted two years ago. (that)

4. I want to see the movie. It is playing at our local theater. (that)

5. Linda won first prize. She is a fine swimmer. (who)

Objective To recognize noun clauses and understand how they are used in sentences

Presenting the Lesson 1. Read the definition of a noun clause and study the examples of noun clauses on page 417. Go over the words on the top of page 418 which commonly introduce noun clauses.

2. Study the examples of diagrams of noun clauses on pages 418 and 419. Point out that the noun clause is placed on a bridge above the main clause. Remind students that adjective and adverb clauses were diagrammed on a line below the words they modified.

3. Assign and discuss Exercises A and B on pages 419 and 420.

Optional Practice Have students complete the following complex sentences by adding words to form noun clauses.

1. Do you know why _____.
2. Whoever _____ is welcome.
3. I have never understood how _____.
4. The volunteers did whatever _____.
5. The surprise is that _____.

Part 7 **A Review of Subordinate Clauses** pp. 420–421

Objective To be able to identify noun, adverb, and adjective subordinate clauses

Presenting the Lesson 1. Read page 420. Remind students that noun, adverb, and adjective clauses are all subordinate clauses. When they occur with a main clause, they form a complex sentence. Review the uses of each kind of clause:

> Noun clauses may be used as:
> subject
> direct object
> object of preposition
> predicate noun
> Adjective clauses may be used to:
> modify nouns
> modify pronouns

Adverb clauses may be used to:
modify verbs
modify adverbs
modify adjectives

Have students recall and state some of the words which commonly introduce the three kinds of clauses.

2. Do exercise A on page 420 orally with the class.
3. Assign and discuss Exercise B on page 421.

Optional Practice Have students tell whether each of the following subordinate clauses is a noun, adverb, or adjective clause. Have students add main clauses to each to make a complex sentence.

1. whoever spilled the Coke
2. that I found in the basement
3. what Jeff would like
4. when the cheering died down
5. that I don't have enough money
6. since the price of gasoline went up
7. where the car keys are
8. whatever she wants
9. as soon as the paramedics arrived
10. who won the most valuable player award

Part 8 **More About Sentence Fragments**   pp. 421–423

Objective To be able to recognize and correct subordinate clause sentence fragments

Presenting the Lesson 1. Read pages 421 and 422. Stress that a subordinate clause is dependent upon the main clause to complete its meaning. A subordinate clause is always incomplete unless it is attached to a main clause. Study the examples of subordinate clauses written as fragments on page 422.

2. Do Exercise A on page 422 as a class activity. Have students identify fragments as noun, adverb, or adjective clauses.

3. Assign and discuss Exercise B on pages 422 and 423.

Extending the Lesson Have students rewrite the following paragraph, correcting the fragments. Students should be able to explain how fragments were corrected.

Paul Zindel is an author of teen fiction. Whom I really admire. I always read his novels. As soon as the library gets them. Because Zindel has a good sense of humor. His characters are always enjoyable to read about. My parents laugh. When I tell them the names of some of Zindel's books. My favorites are *Pardon Me, You're Stepping On My Eyeball* and *The Undertaker's Gone Bananas*. Which I highly recommend.

Part 9 **A Review of Sentences** pp. 423–424

Objective To review simple, compound, and complex sentences

Presenting the Lesson 1. Read page 423, reviewing definitions and examples of simple, compound, and complex sentences. Remind students of certain identifying traits of compound sentences (comma plus coordinating conjunction, or semicolon) and complex sentences (subordinate conjunctions, relative pronouns, certain words such as *that, where, whoever*).

2. Do Exercise A on page 424 as a class activity. Have students identify subjects and verbs in each sentence to aid in determining if the sentence is simple, complex, or compound.

3. Assign and discuss Exercise B on page 424.

Optional Practice Have students take each of the following simple sentences and expand and rewrite them twice, first as a compound sentence and then as a complex sentence.

1. I wore my new boots.

2. "Monday Night Football" is Greg's favorite show.

3. Solar energy will be important in the future.

4. The airlines are raising their fares again.

5. Glenn will make a good salesman.

Review pp. 425–426

You may use the Review on pages 425 and 426 either as a checkup or for additional practice.

Capitalization

Objectives

1. To understand and apply the rules for capitalizing proper nouns and adjectives
2. To understand and apply the rules for capitalizing the first words in sentences, poems, direct quotations, greetings in letters, outlines, and titles

Preparing the Students

Discuss with students how they have been learning about proper word order and patterns to form different kinds of sentences. The arrangement of words and the combinations of words used, communicate very specific information to the reader. To make these patterns even more exact, capitalization and punctuation are used to guide the reader through the written material.

This section will discuss the rules for capitalization. The following section will deal with punctuation.

Proper Nouns and Adjectives

Objective To understand and apply the rules for capitalizing proper nouns and adjectives

Presenting the Lesson 1. Read pages 427 and 428 defining proper nouns and proper adjectives. Ask students to give proper nouns for these words:

boy	magazine	teacher
car	county	river

ask students to form proper adjectives from these words:

Japan	England	France

2. Read pages 428–429. Go over rules and examples, asking students to supply additional examples to go with each rule.

3. Assign and discuss Exercises A and B on pages 429 and 430. In

159

going over exercises, explain why capitalized words need to be capitalized.

4. Read pages 430 and 431. Go over rules and examples, again asking students to supply additional examples.

5. Assign and discuss Exercises A and B on pages 431 and 432.

6. Read pages 432–434. Go over rules and examples. Have students suggest more names of locally familiar organizations and institutions which should be capitalized.

7. Assign and discuss Exercises A and B on pages 434 and 435.

Optional Practice Have students capitalize words where necessary in the following paragraph. For each capital inserted, students should be prepared to tell what rule governs the capitalization.

> my mother and father and i are going to visit aunt esther in london, england, this summer. we will drive east to new york, stopping in the ohio town where i was born. i hope to visit dawes school where i went to first and second grade. i think dr. sawyer, the principal, is still there. then we will fly on a concorde. it will take us less time to cross the atlantic ocean than to get from here to ohio. we will spend all of july with my aunt, and then tour the english countryside in a rented car—probably a german volkswagen—during august.

First Words
pp. 435–438

Objective To understand and apply the rules for capitalizing the first words in sentences, poems, direct quotations, greetings in letters, outlines, and titles

Presenting the Lesson 1. Read pages 435–437. Go over rules and examples. Be sure students understand what a divided quotation is and that the second part is capitalized only when it begins a new sentence.

2. Assign and discuss Exercises A and B on pages 437–438.

Optional Practice Have students insert capital letters where necessary in the following outline.

> readings in english literature
> I. works by william shakespeare
>   A. *romeo and juliet*
>   B. *the taming of the shrew*
>   C. *a comedy of errors*

II. works by dr. samuel johnson
III. works by thomas hardy
    A. novels
       1. *the mayor of casterbridge*
       2. *the return of the native*
    B. poems
       1. "are you digging on my grave"
       2. "during wind and rain"

Extending the Lesson 1. Have students clip out an article from a newspaper or magazine and underline all capitalized words. On a separate sheet of paper, students should list capitalized words and tell why each needs to be capitalized.

2. Have students write a composition based on a current news story giving background as well as the present situation. Have students apply all rules of capitalization covered in Section 13.

Review p. 439

You may use the Review on page 439 either as a checkup or for additional practice.

HANDBOOK SECTION 14

Punctuation Pages 440–466

Objectives

1. To use end marks—periods, question marks, exclamation points—correctly
2. To use the comma correctly
3. To use the semicolon and the colon correctly
4. To use the hyphen correctly
5. To use the apostrophe correctly
6. To use quotation marks correctly

Preparing the Students

Tell students that good driving depends upon understanding and obeying road signs. Road signs tell the driver to stop, to go slowly, to be wary. Good written communication depends upon proper use and understanding of punctuation. Punctuation functions as "road signs" for the reader, telling him or her when to stop, pause, or be prepared for a quotation. Since a reader can't rely on your voice, intonation, or facial gestures, you must use punctuation properly to help convey your meaning fully.

Read the introduction on page 440.

End Marks
pp. 440–443

Objective To use end marks—periods, question marks, exclamation points—correctly

Presenting the Lesson 1. Read page 441 to the top of page 442. Go over rules for using the period. Study examples of the uses of the period. Be certain that students understand the meaning of: *declarative sentence, imperative sentence, indirect question, abbreviation,* and *initials.*

2. Read page 442 and the top of 443 covering the use of the question mark and the exclamation point. Be certain that students understand the meaning of: *interrogative sentence, exclamatory sentence,* and *interjection.* Stress the difference between direct questions and indirect questions. Ask students for examples of each kind of question.

3. Assign and discuss Exercises A and B on page 443.

Optional Practice Have students copy the following sentences, adding the necessary punctuation.

1. Do you ever drink grapefruit juice in the morning
2. Can anyone help unload the station wagon
3. What a horrible mess I'm in
4. The streets were dark and deserted
5. Mac asked Mary if she had seen that movie

Extending the Lesson Have students write and punctuate sentences which do the following:

1. Two sentences describing your best friend

2. Two sentences asking someone to contribute to a local charity

3. Two sentences reacting to a car accident

4. Two sentences telling what your life's ambition is

5. Two sentences containing things you would ask the President if he came to your school

The Comma

pp. 444–452

Objective   To use the comma correctly

Presenting the Lesson   1. Read page 444. Go over the rules and examples showing commas used in series.

2. Assign and discuss Exercises A and B on pages 444 and 445.

3. Read the bottom of page 445 and top of page 446. Be certain that students understand what is meant by *introductory words, phrases, clauses,* and *interrupters.*

4. Assign and discuss Exercises A and B on pages 446 and 447.

5. Read pages 447–449. Be certain that students understand the meaning of a *noun of direct address,* an *appositive,* a *direct quotation,* and a *divided quotation.* Go over rules for punctuating divided quotations carefully. Review the compound sentence and the use of a comma before the conjunction. Stress that a comma does not precede the conjunction in compound sentence parts.

6. Assign and discuss Exercises A and B on pages 449 and 450.

7. Read pages 450 and 451.

8. Assign and discuss Exercises A and B on pages 451 and 452.

Optional Practice   Present the following sentences on the board or on a worksheet. Number the commas as indicated. Have students number their papers from 1–10 and write an explanation for the use of each comma.

1. I don't like disco music,¹ but I like rock,² jazz,³ and classical music.

2. Yes,⁴ Kathy,⁵ the inscription read June 16,⁶ 1980,⁷ the day of her graduation.

163

3. "The problems of the past decade,[8] I predict,[9] will be solved by our youth,[10]" said the senator.

Extending the Lesson Have students write and punctuate sentences which do the following:

1. Two sentences describing the contents of your purse or pocket and your locker
2. Two sentences giving the birthdates of members of your family and important dates in your life
3. Two quotations spoken by a politician or movie star
4. Two addresses of out-of-town friends or relatives
5. Two compound sentences telling what you do in your spare time

The Semicolon and the Colon

pp. 452–455

Objective To use the semicolon and the colon correctly

Presenting the Lesson 1. Read page 452 and the top of 453. Go over rules and examples of the use of semicolons.
2. Read page 453. Go over rules and examples of the use of colons.
3. Assign and discuss Exercises A and B on pages 454 and 455.

Optional Practice Have students insert semicolons or colons where needed in the following sentences. Students should be prepared to explain why each added mark is required.

1. I found the first movie fascinating the second one I didn't care for.
2. The box contained the following items, gauze, iodine, adhesive tape, splints, and elastic bandages.
3. Strep bacteria are very contagious moreover, they can lead to heart damage.
4. Dear Sirs I will arrive in your city at 1000 A.M. Sunday however, I will be leaving at 2:00 P.M.
5. Kate's travels took her to Denver, Colorado Springs, and Aspen, Colorado Albuquerque and Santa Fe, New Mexico and Flagstaff Phoenix and Tucson Arizona.

The Hyphen

pp. 455–456

Objective To use the hyphen correctly

Presenting the Lesson 1. Read pages 455 and 456. Go over rules and examples of the use of the hyphen. Stress that the dictionary should be consulted to check the proper syllable divisions of words. Be certain that students understand the meaning of compound nouns and compound adjectives. Again, students should check the dictionary for the correct use of hyphens in compound nouns and adjectives.

2. Assign and discuss the exercise on page 456.

Optional Practice Have students insert hyphens correctly in the following sentences. Students should consult the dictionary as necessary.

1. Bus fare is fifty five cents.
2. Gloria won three fourths of the games she played.
3. Two thirds of the voters were under forty five years of age.
4. The ready to use frosting isn't nearly as creamy as the homemade kind.
5. Our typing teacher told us to divide the word *instructions* in this way: in struc tions.

The Apostrophe

pp. 457–459

Objective To use the apostrophe correctly

Presenting the Lesson 1. Read page 457 and the top of page 458. Go over rules and examples of the use of the apostrophe to form possessives. Study examples of contractions formed with the use of an apostrophe. Go over rules and examples for using an apostrophe to show omission of numbers in a date and to form plurals of letters, figures, and words used as words.

2. Assign and discuss Exercises A and B on pages 458 and 459.

Optional Practice 1. Have students form the possessive of the following words.

coach	women	Martha	eagle	everyone
Chris	clerks	child	somebody	

2. Have students form contractions from the following words.

I will	they have	he had
she has	could not	I am
it is	is not	you are
have not	will not	does not

Quotation Marks

pp. 459–464

Objective To use quotation marks correctly

Presenting the Lesson 1. Read pages 459 and 460. Review the terms *direct quotation, indirect quotation, explanatory words,* and *divided quotations.* Stress correct placement of commas, periods, and capitals, as well as quotation marks.

2. Do the exercise on page 460 as a class activity. Have quotations written on the board and discuss correct punctuation for each.

3. Read the bottom of page 460 and the top of 461. Study rules and examples of placement of question marks and exclamation points in quotations.

4. Assign and discuss Exercise A on page 461.

5. Assign Exercise B on page 462. Have students volunteer to put their quotations on the board. Try to have several versions for each quote written on the board.

6. Assign and discuss Exercise C on page 462.

7. Read pages 462 and 463. Study rules and examples of other uses of quotation marks.

8. Assign and discuss Exercises A and B on pages 463 and 464.

Extending the Lesson Have students write quotations that do the following:

1. Two quotations that ask a friend if he or she likes a particular song or television program
2. Two quotations that ask directions to a local restaurant
3. Two or more quotations of a dialogue between parents who are upset by something their teen-ager did

Review

p. 465–466

You may use the Review on pages 465–466 either as a checkup or for additional practice.

Spelling

Objectives

1. To develop an effective method to improve spelling skills
2. To develop an effective method to master the spelling of particularly difficult words
3. To understand and apply common spelling rules
4. To become familiar with the use and spelling of words often confused

Preparing the Students

Ask students if they know what the saying "Clothes make the man" means. Explain that often people judge other people by appearance. First impressions say a lot. Poor spelling makes a statement about the writer. To make the best impression possible, good spelling habits should be developed. Some people are better spellers than others, but everyone can benefit from paying closer attention to developing good spelling habits. Read the introduction on page 467.

How To Become a Better Speller

pp. 467–468

Objective To develop an effective method to improve spelling skills

Presenting the Lesson Read the six steps to becoming a better speller on pages 467 and 468. Discuss each step and have students consider how they personally can use and benefit from each step.

Extending the Lesson Have students look at one of their recently written and graded composition assignments. Students should follow steps 1–5 in going over the assignment. Frequently misspelled words should be considered spelling demons and should be given special attention.

How To Master the Spelling of Particular Words
p. 468

Objective To develop an effective method to master the spelling of particular words

Presenting the Lesson 1. Read and discuss the five steps listed on page 468.

2. Have the class practice using the five-step system with some difficult words, such as *exercise, possible, government, chemistry,* and *whether.*

Extending the Lesson Have students list five or more of their own spelling demons; demons can be derived from written assignments. Students should apply the five-step approach to each demon until they have mastered the words.

Rules for Spelling
pp. 469–473

Objective To understand and apply common spelling rules

Presenting the Lesson 1. The rules in this section should be presented as separate lessons over several days' time. Practice with words that apply to each rule as frequently as possible. Before introducing new words and rules, review the previous ones.

2. Read the rules governing the addition of prefixes and the final silent *e* on page 469. Go over examples of words used to illustrate each rule. Be certain that students know the meanings of words before and after the addition of prefixes and suffixes. Check that students can distinguish between suffixes beginning with vowels and those beginning with consonants. Look at and discuss exceptions to the rule regarding retaining the silent *e* on page 469.

3. Assign and discuss Exercises A and B on pages 469 and 470.

4. Read the rules governing words ending in *y* on pages 470 and 471. Stress that the addition of *-ing* constitutes an exception to the rule for changing *y* to *i*. Go over examples of words which conform to the rules and their exceptions. Have students suggest other words ending in *y*. Write them on the board. Add suffixes to each and rewrite the newly formed words in two columns: those in which *y* changes to *i* and those in which *y* does not change. Have students relate the rules on page 470 to the examples on the board.

5. Assign and discuss the exercise on page 471.

6. Read the rules on page 471 governing the suffixes -ness and -ly and the doubling of final consonants. Go over examples. Have students suggest more examples and apply the rules to each.

7. Assign and discuss Exercise A on page 472. As students correct misspelled words, have them state the rule which governs the correction.

8. Read the rules on pages 472 and 473 governing words with the "seed" sound and words with ie and ei. Study examples.

9. Assign and discuss the exercise on page 473.

Optional Practice Dictate the following words to the class. Have them spell the words correctly.

1. tripping	10. skating	18. famous
2. succeed	11. misspell	19. silliest
3. niece	12. truly	20. reelect
4. hurrying	13. equally	21. unnatural
5. marrying	14. thinness	22. naturally
6. marriage	15. easily	23. hopping
7. lazier	16. slipped	24. hoping
8. relation	17. shining	25. precede
9. hateful		

Extending the Lesson Play the following game with students. Have students number their papers from 1–10. Tell them you will read the name of a rule and a sentence containing a blank. Each blank can be filled with a word which illustrates the use of one of the rules in this section. After the proper number, students should write the word which fills the blank. The winner is the student who supplies and correctly spells all ten words.

Words with the "seed" sound

1. The price of gasoline cannot _____ a certain price posted on the pump. (exceed)

Words with ie and ei

2. In order to wear certain earrings, you must _____ your ears. (pierce)

3. People retire to the sunbelt to spend their _____ time enjoying warm weather. (leisure)

4. You must have a cash register _____ in order to return your gift. (receipt)

Words ending in *y*

5. Do the ＿＿＿＿ problems first and save the hardest ones for later. (easiest)

The suffixes *-ness* and *-ly*

6. Mother never gets angry; she always displays ＿＿＿＿ of temper. (evenness)

Doubling the final consonant

7. The tire marks showed that the car ＿＿＿＿ before it hit the guard rail. (skidded)

The addition of prefixes

8. It is ＿＿＿＿ to drive through a red light. (illegal)

The final silent *e*

9. The pitcher is the ＿＿＿＿, or last, batter in the batting order. (ninth)

10. Write a thank-you note to show how ＿＿＿＿ you are for the kindness shown to you. (grateful)

Words Often Confused

pp. 473–476

Objective To become familiar with the use and spelling of words often confused

Presenting the Lesson 1. Explain that this section presents sets of words which are often confused, and consequently misspelled, because they sound the same. They are called *homonyms*. Tell the students that the key to proper usage and spelling of these words is to understand the differences in meaning and spelling in each set.

2. For each of the twelve sets of words, read the definitions and carefully note the differences in spelling. Have students use each word in each set in a sentence.

3. Offer certain tricks to help students distinguish between words often confused. For example:

a capit*ol* is a building with a d*o*me
a princi*pal* is your *pal*
station*ery* is made out of pap*er*

Ask students to think up some helpful sayings of their own to help with the words in this section.

4. Assign and discuss Exercises A and B on pages 475 and 476.

Optional Practice   Have students fill the blanks in the following sentences with the correct homonyms.

1. Dan will _____ the race because his skates are too _____. (loose, lose)

2. _____ running as fast as _____ legs can carry them. (they're, their, there)

3. The group did not want to _____ their friend in the _____. (dessert, desert)

4. Can everyone _____ _____ the speaker? (hear, here)

5. I don't know _____ the _____ will improve or not. (weather, whether)

6. As a matter of _____, the student took his complaint to the _____. (principle, principal)

7. Do you want _____ swim or is it _____ cold? (too, two, to)

8. In the _____ building in Texas they are debating _____ punishment. (capital, Capitol, capitol)

9. _____ easy to see why the restaurant lost _____ steady customers. (it's, its)

10. _____ going to decide _____ turn it is? (whose, who's)

Review

p. 477

You may use the Review on page 477 either as a checkup or for additional practice.

The Correct Form for Writing
Pages 478–484

Objectives

1. To use legible handwriting and to produce a neat, correct final copy
2. To become acquainted with accepted forms for headings, titles, margins, and spacing
3. To use numbers correctly in writing
4. To use abbreviations correctly in writing

Preparing the Students

Read the introduction on page 478. Stress that while *what* you say is most important, *how* you present your material also affects communication with your reader.

Legible Writing p. 479

Objective   To use legible handwriting and to produce a neat, correct final copy

Presenting the Lesson   Read page 479. Discuss the importance of taking care to write neatly and to proofread carefully. Discuss the advantages of writing a rough draft and doing revisions of that draft. Explain that good proofreading uncovers errors in spelling and punctuation and also errors in meaning caused by words left out or written incorrectly.

Extending the Lesson   Have each student write a one-page composition. Any topic may be used, or students may use one of these titles:

> Everyone Needs a Friend Sometimes
> Television Can Be Educational
> Safety Belts Save Lives
> My Hero Is Not a Famous Person
> Teenagers Can Teach Adults

Students should write a rough draft and make revisions. A final copy should be written. After a day or two has elapsed, students should

172

proofread and make note of errors discovered. You may also want students to exchange papers for a second proofreading.

The Correct Form

pp. 479–480

Objective To become acquainted with accepted forms for headings, titles, margins, and spacing

Presenting the Lesson Read pages 479 and 480. Go over the accepted format as suggested, and modify or supplement with your own standards of form. If possible, have several properly arranged pages for students to see as examples of accepted form.

Numbers in Writing

pp. 481–482

Objective To use numbers correctly in writing

Presenting the Lesson 1. Read page 481. Go over rules for the use of numbers. Study sample sentences illustrating when figures are used and when numbers are spelled out.
2. Assign and discuss the exercise on page 482.

Optional Practice Have students write ten sentences of their own using as many numbers as possible. Students should be prepared to explain why each number is written as it is.

Abbreviations in Writing

pp. 482–484

Objective To use abbreviations correctly in writing

Presenting the Lesson 1. Read pages 482 and 483. Go over rules and examples showing correct usage of abbreviations.
2. Assign and discuss the exercise on page 483. Students should explain why each correction was needed.
3. Read page 484 regarding ZIP codes and state abbreviations.

Optional Practice Have students write ten sentences using abbreviations correctly. Several should include names and addresses of local doctors, dentists, religious, or government officials.

Basic Skills in English

BOOK 4

COMPOSITION

Building Your Vocabulary

(Definitions and word derivations are based on
*Webster's New World Dictionary of the American Language,
Students' Edition.*)

Page 3, Check It Out

1. basset—a kind of hunting hound with a long body, short legs, and long drooping ears; *like* signals an example
2. enigmatic—of or like an enigma; puzzling; mysterious; *or* signals restatement
3. griffin—a mythical animal, part lion and part eagle; definition
4. resumed—to begin again or go on again after interruption; *but* signals a contrast

Page 4, Check It Out

Melancholy is a sad or depressed mood; pensiveness.

Page 5, Try Your Skill

1. eclectic—made up of parts chosen from various sources
2. spontaneous combustion—the catching on fire of matter as a result of heat built up in it by slow oxidation
3. amphitheatre—a round or oval building with an open space (arena) surrounded by rising rows of seats

Page 7, Check It Out

1. *Modern* is the best synonym for *new* because it suggests that they are the most recent and up-to-date appliances. *Fresh* would be used to refer to something new but natural or organic. *Novel* refers to something new and unusual; *original* refers to the first or earliest of its kind.
2. *Noisy* is the best synonym for *loud* because it suggests full of noise in contrast to the library's quiet. The other three words go beyond suggesting sound and describe feelings or moods as well. *Exciting* suggests a thrilling atmosphere; *confusing* suggests disorder or bewilderment; and *disagreeable*, an unpleasantness.

Page 7, Try Your Skill

1. I want you to be honest with me, even if it hurts me. dishonest
2. My father was extremely strict, but he was fair. lenient
3. The two tug-of-war teams pulled the rope taut. slack

Page 9, Check It Out

prefix — *in-*; base word—*active*
prefix — *il-*; base word—*logical*
prefix — *im-*; base word—*possible*
prefix — *ir-*; base word—*responsible*
prefix — *mis-*; base word—*judge*

prefix — *pre-*; base word—*view*
prefix — *re-*; base word—*write*
prefix — *sub-*; base word—*standard*
prefix — *super-*; base word—*human*

Page 9, Try Your Skill

1. less than + human
2. wrong + pronounce
3. not + adequate
4. no prefix
5. before + heat
6. more than + market
7. no prefix
8. less than + atomic
9. more than + fine
10. again + run
11. again + marry
12. not + resistable
13. before + pay
14. bad + treat
15. no prefix

Page 11, Check It Out

suffix — *-able*; base word—*enjoy*
suffix — *-ible*; base word—*sense*
suffix — *-er*; base word—*amplify*
suffix — *-or*; base word—*counsel*

suffix — *-ist*; base word—*alarm*
suffix — *-less*; base word—*effort*
suffix — *-ful*; base word—*tact*
suffix — *-ous*; base word—*grace*

Page 11, Try Your Skill

1. care + without
2. race + person that does something
3. biology + person who does something
4. comfort + having this quality
5. tear + full of
6. courage + full of
7. power + without
8. manage + having this quality
9. doubt + full of
10. terror + person who does something
11. operate + person that does something
12. pity + full of
13. religion + full of
14. accept + having this quality
15. glory + full of

Page 13, Check It Out

dictate: root—*dict*
contradict: root—*dict*
export: root—*port*
report: root—*port*

inscribe: root—*scrib*
prescription: root—*script*
invisible: root—*vis*

Page 13, Try Your Skill

dictionary: root—*dict*; a book of words in a language with their definitions
dictator: root—*dict*; a ruler with absolute authority
import: root—*port*; to bring in from the outside
transport: root—*port*; to carry from one place to another
script: root—*script*; handwriting; a copy of the text of a play or movie
describe: root—*scrib*; to tell or write about
television: root—*vis*; the process of sending pictures by radio waves

Improving Your Sentences

Page 23, Check It Out

1. unrelated detail—and Columbus is the capital
2. unrelated detail—who has a new girlfriend
3. unrelated detail—which is a huge continent
4. unrelated detail—which was built two years ago

Page 23, Try Your Skill   (The following are sample sentence revisions.)

1. Owls can see well at night.
2. Abraham Lincoln delivered the Gettysburg Address in 1863.
3. My grandfather, who is eighty years old, said that he can remember a time when there were no cars.
4. New York City is one of the world's most important centers of business and culture.

Page 25, Check It Out   (The following are sample sentence revisions.)

1. unsupported opinion
   In order to be self-sufficient, everyone should learn to cook a few basic meals.
2. repeats an idea
   I like loud music because I find it exhilarating.
3. unsupported opinion
   A dog makes the best pet because dogs enjoy running and playing with their owners.
4. unsupported opinion
   High schools should teach driver's education because learning to drive is an important part of every student's education.

Page 25, Try Your Skill   (The following are sample sentence revisions.)

1. Like all natural resources, food should not be wasted.
2. I enjoy playing the piano because I enjoy learning about music.
3. People should drive smaller cars because they generally use fuel more efficiently.
4. Fishing is the most enjoyable hobby because it is relaxing and also provides good food.

Page 27, Check It Out   (These are sample sentence revisions.)

1. I do not have enough money.
2. Jackie had to work late because the restaurant was very busy.
3. Because I enjoy photography, I bought a camera.
4. Since our cat likes to prowl, it sometimes disappears for days.

Page 27, Try Your Skill   (These are sample sentence revisions.)

1. Sheila needed a ride.
2. Every morning I drink orange juice.
3. Since Paul missed the beginning of the movie, he did not understand the ending.
4. My first view of the ocean was from my grandparents' home on the Maine coast.

Page 29, Try Your Skill   (These are sample sentence revisions.)

1. In my uncle's garage are several old license plates, some bald tires, and his trash barrels. There is so much junk that he cannot fit his car into the garage.
2. With the score tied 103 to 103, Jones brought the ball up the court and passed to Russo. There were only three seconds left to play. Russo took a jumpshot and scored the winning basket right at the buzzer.
3. We ran into the water. I knew right away the undertow was strong. I shouted to Ben and Betty, but both of them told me not to worry.

What Is a Paragraph?

Page 35, Try Your Skill

Main idea: The Galápagos Islands are a mysterious and unusual place.

2. The group of fifteen islands was once known as the Enchanted Isles.
3. Pirates buried treasure on these islands.
5. These strange islands take their name from the Spanish word for the huge turtles that live there.
7. The unusual animals that live on these islands include four-foot-long lizards called *iguanas*.

Page 37, Try Your Skill

1. We surprised my sister Diane on her sixteenth birthday.
2. A breed of dog that is not commonly seen as a pet is the Afghan hound.
3. By making popcorn, you have created the perfect late night snack.

The Narrative Paragraph

Page 73, Try Your Skill

d, c, a, b, e

The Explanatory Paragraph

Page 89, Try Your Skill

How To Cook an Omelet
1. Break three eggs into a small mixing bowl.
2. Add one tablespoon of water and a pinch of salt to the eggs.
3. Beat the eggs, water, and salt until the mixture is light and foamy.
4. Pour the beaten eggs into a hot, greased skillet.

5. Stir the eggs clockwise with a fork while gently shaking the skillet.
6. When the eggs are set on the bottom, fold the omelet in half.
7. Flip the cooked omelet onto a warm platter.

How To Make a Clay Pot
1. Center a lump of wet clay on a potter's wheel.
2. Use the movement of the spinning potter's wheel to shape the clay into a pot.
3. Let the wet clay pot dry for several days.
4. Paint the dry clay pot with a glaze.
5. Fire the glazed pot in an oven.

Using the Library

Page 188, Try Your Skill

1. *Julie of the Wolves*—G
   Rumble-Fish—H
   Where the Lilies Bloom—C
   Bless the Beasts and Children—S
   Listen for the Fig Tree—M

2. the poetry of Emily Dickinson—800–899
   practical uses of geometry—500–599
   how Congress works—300–399
   the Spanish language—400–499
   what to visit in New York City—900–999

Page 194, Try Your Skill

1. Nevada
2. television
3. Confederate States
4. Brazil
5. Danube River
6. Johnson, Samuel
7. Kansas
8. paint
9. peanuts
10. painting

Page 197, Try Your Skill

1. atlas
2. almanac; *Readers' Guide*
3. vertical file
4. atlas
5. yearbook; almanac
6. *Readers' Guide*
7. biographical reference

The Sentence and Its Parts

Page 236, Exercise A

1. S	5. S	9. S
2. F	6. S	10. S
3. F	7. F	
4. S	8. F	

Page 237, Exercise B

1. F	5. S	9. S
2. S	6. F	10. S
3. F	7. F	
4. S	8. S	

Page 238, Exercise A

	Subject	Predicate
1.	Gayle	made spaghetti with meatballs.
2.	The Packers	will play the Bears on Sunday.
3.	Beth	walked home with Jenny.
4.	My parents	were fishing from the bridge.
5.	Heavy white smoke	came out of the chimney.
6.	Dracula	is probably the most famous vampire.
7.	I	like science fiction.
8.	Rebecca	learned self-defense last summer.
9.	The sport of rugby	is very rugged.
10.	Rugby	is a British sport similar to our football.

Page 238, Exercise B

	Subject	Predicate
1.	Monarch butterflies	migrate every year.
2.	Sugar cane	is the chief product of Hawaii.
3.	North Dakota	produces barley, wheat, and flaxseed.
4.	Kathy	ate all the pizza.
5.	The bike-a-thon	raised money for muscular dystrophy.
6.	Our homeroom	will play intramural hockey tomorrow.
7.	"Mork and Mindy"	is my favorite TV show.
8.	My friend Tim	built a lamp with scrap wood.
9.	Photography	is Elizabeth's main interest.
10.	Our 4-H Club	showed black angus cattle at the State Fair.

Page 240, Exercise A

	Verb	Subject
1.	arrived	Oranges
2.	printed	computer
3.	rocked	balloon
4.	has	bike
5.	rose	crowd
6.	sank	center
7.	belongs	locker
8.	won	Laura
9.	is	woman
10.	fought	pirate

Page 241, Exercise B

	Verb	Subject
1.	trotted	horse
2.	drifted	sailboat
3.	leads	corridor
4.	wandered	player
5.	suggests	booklet
6.	started	spark
7.	explained	show
8.	assisted	driver
9.	paralyzed	snow
10.	reduced	drought

Page 243, Exercise A

1. have gone
2. has been completed
3. do arrive
4. have been
5. did see
6. will arrive
7. has jammed
8. is going
9. may have been delivered
10. was passing

Page 243, Exercise B

1. are giving
2. do like
3. was approaching
4. will finish
5. has rained
6. was
7. was walking
8. have planted
9. made
10. had collected

Page 244, Exercise A

	Subject	Verb	Use of *there*
1.	he	goes	adverb
2.	trophy	stood	adverb
3.	they	are	adverb
4.	practice	will be	introductory word
5.	runners	go	adverb
6.	I	sat	adverb
7.	I	waited	adverb
8.	picnic	will be	introductory word
9.	pause	was	introductory word
10.	races	will be	introductory word

Page 245, Exercise B

	Subject	Verb	Use of *there*
1.	runner	goes	adverb
2.	pie	is	introductory word
3.	school	will be	introductory word
4.	lock	is	adverb
5.	exits	are	introductory word
6.	thunderstorm	might be	introductory word
7.	rehearsal	is	introductory word
8.	wind	came	introductory word
9.	assembly	will be	introductory word
10.	students	are	introductory word

Page 247, Exercise A

	Subject	Verb
1.	(you)	Hang
2.	minutes	are left
3.	you	Did read
4.	Economy	is
5.	Angela	raced
6.	rain	came
7.	team	is
8.	bus	comes
9.	plants	hung
10.	you	Have seen

Page 247, Exercise B

	Subject	Verb
1.	books	Are
2.	sun	came
3.	T-shirts	are
4.	you	Have heard
5.	swimmers	basked
6.	people	emerged
7.	reply	came
8.	(you)	Do stand
9.	mail	comes
10.	you	Do like

Page 249, Exercise

2. Direct Object
5. Direct Object
6. Direct Object
8. Direct Object
10. Direct Object

Page 250, Exercise A

	Verb	Indirect Object	Direct Object
1.	brought	Cindy	book
2.	gave	parents	scare
3.	made	us	dinner
4.	gave	chili	stir
5.	hooked	Mom	rug
6.	gave	co-captains	trophy
7.	Will bring	me	ice
8.	sparkled		
9.	must have ironed		shirt
10.	got		watch

Page 250, Exercise B

	Verb	Indirect Object	Direct Object
1.	cleaned		courtyard
2.	loaned	me	thesaurus
3.	warned		Paula
4.	were whistling		song
5.	gave		cactus
6.	Did buy	me	film
7.	shouted		
8.	Did align		wheels
9.	get	me	stamps
10.	repaired		steps

Page 253, Exercise A

	Subject	Linking Verb	Predicate Word
1.	Snakes	are	reptiles
2.	song	sounded	good
3.	This	is	he
4.	flowers	looked	dry
5.	Kathy	Has been	sick
6.	driver	was	angry
7.	house	seemed	empty
8.	Karen	felt	lonesome
9.	it	Was	she
10.	Sue	became	chairperson

Page 253, Exercise B

	Subject	Verb	Direct Object	Predicate Word
1.	Tracey Miles	is		designer
2.	Tracey	is		skillful
3.	She	plans	design	
4.	cover	is		idea
5.	She	illustrates	articles	
6.	Tracey	coordinates	work	
7.	Photographs	are used		
8.	Ken Lyle	is		photographer
9.	Tracey	gives	assignments	
10.	magazine	is		slick

Page 255, Exercise A

1. cool, clear—compound predicate words
2. skated, swam—compound verbs
3. hesitated, purred—compound verbs

4. Tara, Charlene—compound subjects
5. Daisy, I—compound subjects; washed, waxed—compound verbs
6. Fritos, popcorn—compound objects
7. posters, flyers—compound objects
8. Marla, Jeff—compound subjects
9. balloons, decorations, prizes—compound objects
10. discipline, skill, control—compound objects

Page 255, Exercise B   (Sentences will vary.)

1. Jon carried the groceries and packages into the house.
2. The pizza was spicy and thick!
3. Did you remember the Kleenex and the paper towels?
4. There are pickles and mustard over here.
5. The hypnotist's performance was phony and laughable.
6. Ms. Lopez gave Jerry a tie and a wallet.
7. Next came the President's car and the Secret Service agents.
8. Linda fixed the handlebars and the seat.
9. Mr. and Mrs. Karnatz gave Meredith and Lauren jobs at the store.
10. There are ten divers and twenty swimmers competing.

Page 257, Exercise A

1. Declarative—Carrie found a summer job.
2. Interrogative—Has the pizza been delivered?
3. Imperative—Please deposit the exact change.
4. Exclamatory—How strong you are!
5. Exclamatory—Wow! We're here at last!
6. Declarative—The rear fender is dented.
7. Exclamatory—Watch out!
8. Interrogative—Do you know shorthand?
9. Imperative—Ask the manager.
10. Declarative—Jamie asked for the car.

Page 257, Exercise B

1. Declarative—I am dieting.
2. Exclamatory—What a terrific idea that is!
3. Interrogative—What is the chef's specialty?
4. Exclamatory—How lucky you are!
5. Interrogative—Have you traveled in the West?
6. Interrogative—Who is the best candidate?
7. Declarative—Ms. Allen is a police dispatcher.
8. Exclamatory—Don't touch that live wire!
9. Interrogative—Does Molly sing in the choir?
10. Imperative—Apply at the main desk.

Subject	Verb
1. cattle	stampeded
2. buses	passed
3. jury	returned
4. players	have signed
5. Jason	will return
6. Ms. Sanders	was joking
7. taxes	are
8. you	Did bring
9. snowplow	came
10. (you)	Take
11. Stacey	operates
12. Garrett	owes
13. Robert Klein	is
14. sky	looks
15. Rachel, Jodie	are

16. Interrogative—Where is the tallest roller coaster?
17. Declarative—Don sells magazine subscriptions.
18. Exclamatory—Stop that racket!
19. Exclamatory—What a great skater she is!
20. Imperative—Check the batteries.

HANDBOOK SECTION 2

Using Complete Sentences

Page 261, Exercise A

1. S	5. F	9. S
2. S	6. F	10. F
3. F	7. S	
4. S	8. F	

Page 261, Exercise B

1. F	5. F	9. S
2. F	6. F	10. S
3. S	7. F	
4. F	8. S	

Page 262, Exercise A

1. Our state has a lottery. The grand prize is one million dollars.
2. Cable television is becoming popular. It offers varied programming.
3. Kristen trains seeing-eye dogs. She enjoys her work.
4. Todd replaced the wiring. Now the doorbell works.
5. Lopez stole third base. Later he scored a homerun.

6. Karen ran the 100 meter dash. She placed second.
7. The pilots waited in the cockpit. They studied the flight plan.
8. Frank's dog was lost. We searched the neighborhood for it.
9. Fuel was scarce. There was talk of gas rationing.
10. Julie studied the math problem. She figured out the right answer.

Page 263, Exercise B

1. Films about outer space use special effects. The results are striking.
2. Julie runs every day. She usually runs six miles.
3. The burglar alarm sounded. No one heard it.
4. The hikers followed mountain trails. They finally reached the peak.
5. Charla breeds Siamese cats. She has eight of them.
6. The committee held a hearing. The topic was new energy sources.
7. Insulation is important for houses. It keeps heat inside during the winter.
8. The scientist made a man-powered airplane. It flies short distances.
9. Reggie put her books in her locker. Then she went to the cafeteria.
10. A drawbridge spans the river. It is raised for tall ships.

Page 264, Review

1. Fragment	6. Run-on	11. Run-on	16. Fragment
2. Sentence	7. Fragment	12. Sentence	17. Run-on
3. Fragment	8. Sentence	13. Fragment	18. Sentence
4. Sentence	9. Fragment	14. Sentence	19. Run-on
5. Run-on	10. Fragment	15. Sentence	20. Run-on

Using Nouns

Page 266, Exercise

Names of Persons	Names of Places	Names of Things	
Chinese	China	earthquake	thousands
	Tientsin	tremors	buildings
	Tangshan	quake	city
		hundreds	mines
		miles	people
		city	lives

Page 267, Exercise A

Common Nouns	Proper Nouns
1. town, city	Salt Lake City, Las Vegas, Atlanta
2. dancer, opera	Maria Tallchief, Joan Sutherland
3. book, magazine	*Reader's Digest, Sports Illustrated, Seventeen*
4. state, region	Montana, Kansas, Indiana
5.	Crater Lake, Gulf of Mexico, Lake Champlain
6. continent, peninsula	Africa, Europe, Korea, Italy
7. track meet, hockey	Olympic Games, Cincinnati Reds, World Series
8. mountain, hills	Andes, Old Smoky
9. artist, sculptor	Georgia O'Keeffe, Alexander Calder
10. monument, building	Mount Rushmore, Statue of Liberty, Empire State Building

Page 267, Exercise B   Sentences will vary.

Page 268, Exercise A

1. soldiers
2. Pineapples
3. natives
4. Brenda
5. Dana
6. Connie
7. Dale, Lee
8. vines
9. cafeteria
10. snakes

Page 269, Exercise B

1. Penny
2. librarians
3. Sally, Shawn
4. Carpenters
5. plants
6. Chief Joseph
7. cloud
8. cost
9. Kathleen, Amy
10. Fruits, vegetables

Page 270, Exercise A

1. groceries
2. sand
3. union
4. crane
5. sign
6. food
7. nest
8. building
9. bushes, hedges
10. roof, gutters

Page 270, Exercise B

1. Frisbee
2. scaffold
3. shells
4. story
5. insurance
6. blisters
7. coats
8. corn, soybeans
9. attic, basement
10. acres

Page 272, Exercise A

1. Judy
2. police
3. Ellen
4. Brad
5. Mel
6. children
7. family
8. grandmother
9. Beth, Alana
10. friends

Page 272, Exercise B

1. Grandma
2. Valerie
3. Natalie
4. Deedee
5. committee
6. Jean
7. Melissa, Don
8. Kara
9. dogs
10. Mom, Dad

Page 273, Exercise A

1. trailer
2. sherbet
3. driver
4. fruit
5. disco
6. actress
7. practices
8. Steve, Lindsay
9. place
10. popcorn, pretzels

Page 274, Exercise B

1. island
2. fleet
3. North Freeway
4. coach
5. fuel
6. writer
7. seats
8. pizza, lasagna
9. diplomats, Senators
10. hangout

Page 276, Exercise A

1. churches
2. brushes
3. elves
4. wishes
5. potatoes
6. dishes
7. wives
8. sheep
9. foxes
10. teeth
11. companies
12. watches
13. bookshelves
14. chimneys
15. ladies
16. babies
17. cities
18. mice
19. witches
20. radios

Page 276, Exercise B

1. We placed all of the dishes on the benches in the hallway.
2. Several different companies make CB radios.
3. The thieves took several loaves of bread.
4. The babies were getting new teeth.
5. Several companies sell frozen mashed potatoes.
6. First, cut the loaves in halves.
7. The deer were eating the green shoots on the bushes.
8. Use these brushes to stain the bookshelves.
9. The larger boxes had scratches on them.
10. My blue jeans are covered with patches.

Page 277, Exercise A

1. bee's
2. Mary's
3. carpenter's
4. child's
5. Martha's
6. princess's
7. mouse's
8. Andrea's
9. watchman's
10. waitress's
11. Thomas's
12. Les's
13. mirror's
14. conductor's
15. Tricia's
16. winner's
17. Tracy's
18. singer's
19. lake's
20. Vince's

1. watchmen's
2. teachers'
3. women's
4. children's
5. people's
6. birds'
7. sheep's
8. schools'
9. boys'
10. ladies'
11. countries'
12. dogs'
13. socks'
14. churches'
15. dresses'
16. stereos'
17. foxes'
18. ducks'
19. engineers'
20. statues'

Page 278, Exercise C

1. class's, teacher's
2. Council's, teachers', principal's
3. Thomas's
4. brother's
5. Maurita's, Amy's
6. farmer's
7. painter's
8. Jonathan's
9. neighbor's
10. Janine's

Page 279, Review

1. towns, Cape Cod, Hyannis, Orleans
2. Robert E. Lee, sword, Appomattox
3. student, town, Leechburg
4. weekends, Josett, Charles, gravel, trucks
5. Massachusetts, Plymouth Rock
6. course—Direct Object
7. dog—Subject
8. police—Indirect Object; story—Direct Object
9. mammals—Predicate Noun
10. Extras—Subject; actors—Predicate Noun
11. bunches
12. tomatoes
13. ponies
14. shelves
15. feet
16. Jenny's
17. Elvis's
18. ladies'
19. planets'
20. people's

HANDBOOK SECTION 4

Using Pronouns

Page 282, Exercise A

1. her (Sue), her (Sue)
2. it (snow)
3. their (John, Ginny)
4. his (Ken)
5. he (alderman), our (the speaker)
6. They (Sierra Nevadas)
7. her (Dorinda)
8. its (station)
9. her (Linda), they (Linda, friend)
10. he (Jay), it (envelope)

Page 282, Exercise B

1. you (person spoken to), me (the speaker)
2. It (seismograph), their (earthquakes)
3. our (the speaker), their (neighbors); my, I (the speaker)
4. They (Joel, Jim Hertz), them (tomatoes)
5. her (Anita), she (Anita), them (jeans)
6. My (the speaker), I (the speaker)
7. you (Mary), your (Mary)
8. his (Bill), them (books)
9. it (sun), They (sun dogs)
10. you (person spoken to), him (noun not stated), we (the speaker)

Page 286, Exercise A

1. him
2. she
3. me
4. them
5. him
6. she
7. they
8. yours
9. he
10. her

Page 287, Exercise B

1. me
2. they
3. theirs
4. me
5. me
6. her
7. us
8. he
9. them
10. I

Page 287, Exercise C

1. him—Object Form
2. us—Object Form
3. you—Object Form
4. They—Subject Form; her—Object Form
5. He—Subject Form; them—Object Form
6. We—Subject Form; him—Object Form
7. us—Object Form
8. me—Object Form
9. us—Object Form
10. she—Subject Form

Page 289, Exercise A

1. she
2. us
3. she
4. me
5. him and me
6. me
7. them and me
8. She
9. she
10. me

Page 289, Exercise B

1. My parents and I are going to the family reunion tonight.
2. Larry and they have gone to Detroit.
3. The telephone must be for either you or her.

4. Everyone except Janet and her had enough money.
5. The packages were divided evenly between Tanya and me.
6. Judy and she just went out the back door.
7. Ms. McGowan made Meg and me a sandwich.
8. The bus driver gave Mary Beth and me directions.
9. Peggy and Linda sat next to Lauri and me at the concert.
10. correct

Page 290, Exercise A

1. boy
2. Kathy, Kathy
3. box
4. people
5. executive
6. Sarah
7. glass
8. Brenda
9. members
10. shelter

Page 291, Exercise B

1. paramedics
2. coat
3. Phil
4. ballpark
5. Mrs. Kohl
6. you
7. Curt
8. Lara, Pete
9. Susie
10. photographer, lenses

Page 292, Exercise A

1. ourselves (We)
2. yourself (you)
3. himself or herself (Bret)
4. themselves (fans)
5. itself (fire)
6. myself (I)
7. ourselves (we)
8. themselves (Nancy, Carrie, Sue)
9. ourselves (We)
10. myself (I)

Page 292, Exercise B

1. itself (door)
2. herself (Diane)
3. yourself (Jamie)
4. ourselves (We)
5. yourselves (you)
6. herself (Bridget)
7. yourselves (you)
8. ourselves (We)
9. itself (store)
10. himself (He)

Page 293, Exercise

1. Those
2. That
3. Those
4. This or That
5. These or Those
6. That
7. These or Those
8. These
9. That
10. That

Page 293, Exercise

1. Those—Demonstrative
2. Which—Interrogative; you
3. This—Demonstrative
4. none
5. What—Interrogative
6. Which—Interrogative
7. themselves
8. Who—Interrogative
9. Which—Interrogative
10. These—Demonstrative

Page 295, Exercise A

1. anything
2. Both
3. All
4. Somebody
5. Either
6. everyone
7. anyone
8. One
9. Each
10. Everyone

Page 295, Exercise B

1. his or her
2. him or her
3. their
4. their
5. his or her
6. his or her
7. their
8. his or her
9. their
10. his or her

Page 296, Exercise C

1. Neither fits
2. few are
3. Some are
4. Each sends
5. Neither explains
6. All were
7. All have
8. Several were
9. Neither was
10. Both work

Page 297, Exercise A

1. its
2. Whose
3. Your
4. they're
5. Who's
6. They're, it's
7. Who's
8. They're, their
9. your
10. Who's

Page 297, Exercise B

1. It is
2. Who is
3. We have
4. Who would
5. They have
6. Who has
7. You have
8. It is
9. *Who Is*
10. When is

Page 298, Exercise A

1. Who
2. Who
3. Who
4. whom
5. whom
6. Who
7. Who
8. Whom
9. Whom
10. whom

Page 299, Exercise B

1. whom
2. whom
3. Who
4. Whom
5. whom
6. Who
7. whom
8. whom
9. whom
10. Who

Page 300, Exercise A

1. those
2. us
3. Those
4. We
5. us
6. those
7. us
8. us
9. those
10. We

Page 300, Exercise B

1. We	3. those	5. Those	7. us	9. We
2. those	4. us	6. We	8. those	10. us

Page 301, Review

1. They
2. she
3. us
4. him
5. me
6. yours
7. I
8. them
9. her
10. ourselves
11. yourself
12. These
13. Which
14. his or her
15. their
16. your
17. whom
18. Who
19. We
20. Those

HANDBOOK SECTION 5

Using Verbs

Page 304, Exercise A

1. smells—Linking
2. taste—Linking
3. appeared—Action
4. looked—Action
5. waited—Action
6. raced—Action
7. look—Linking
8. broke—Action
9. looks—Linking
10. sounds—Linking

Page 305, Exercise B

1. stopped—Transitive
2. went—Intransitive
3. Has quit—Transitive
4. lined—Intransitive
5. paid—Intransitive
6. missed—Transitive
7. produces—Transitive
8. owns—Transitive
9. protested—Intransitive
10. distorts—Transitive

Page 306, Exercise A

	Helping Verb	Main Verb
1.	are	going
2.	have	completed
3.	has	gone
4.	Will	go
5.	must have	snowed
6.	are	going
7.	was	writing
8.	is	running
9.	have	skated
10.	Did	land

Page 307, Exercise B

1.	have been	designed
2.	can	go
3.	is	considered
4.	are	required
5.	are	concerned
6.	has	become
7.	do	conserve
8.	Will	make
9.	can	help
10.	may	heat

Page 309, Exercise A

1. are—present
2. have enjoyed—present perfect
3. walk—present
4. Will come—future
5. Have refereed—present perfect
6. will open—future
7. have traveled—present perfect
8. will have heard—future perfect
9. will open—future
10. has opened—present perfect

Page 309, Exercise B   Sentences will vary.

Page 310, Exercise

Present	Past	Past Participle
1. worry	worried	worried
2. sob	sobbed	sobbed
3. pay	paid	paid
4. carry	carried	carried
5. grab	grabbed	grabbed
6. help	helped	helped
7. pass	passed	passed
8. end	ended	ended
9. slip	slipped	slipped
10. use	used	used
11. rob	robbed	robbed
12. like	liked	liked
13. rap	rapped	rapped
14. hurry	hurried	hurried
15. rub	rubbed	rubbed

Page 313, Exercise A

1. cost	4. said	7. put	9. burst
2. caught	5. led	8. set	10. brought
3. sat	6. lost		

Page 313, Exercise B

1. brought	4. led	7. cost	9. caught
2. caught	5. lost	8. put	10. said
3. set	6. lent		

Page 314, Exercise A

1. frozen
2. wore
3. stole
4. chosen
5. broken
6. tore
7. spoken
8. worn
9. frozen
10. chose

Page 314, Exercise B

1. torn
2. broke
3. stolen
4. spoke
5. worn
6. broke
7. tore
8. chosen
9. stolen
10. spoken

Page 315, Exercise A

1. drank
2. sung
3. begun
4. rang
5. swam
6. began
7. rung
8. swum
9. sang
10. drunk

Page 316, Exercise B

1. sang
2. rung
3. swum
4. drunk
5. began
6. sung
7. rang
8. swam
9. begun
10. drank

Page 317, Exercise A

1. saw
2. came
3. done
4. threw
5. taken
6. grown
7. written
8. fell
9. gone
10. run

Page 317, Exercise B

1. rode
2. known
3. eaten
4. gone
5. given
6. run
7. taken
8. came
9. seen
10. did

Page 321, Exercise A

1. rose
2. rises
3. Leave
4. Leave
5. rose
6. Lie
7. laid
8. rising
9. lie
10. laid

Page 321, Exercise B

1. sit
2. set
3. May
4. May
5. set
6. Teach
7. May
8. sitting
9. could
10. learned

1. waited	15. has watched	29. gone
2. traded	16. set	30. came
3. are	17. lost	31. learned
4. was	18. brought	32. taught
5. won	19. caught	33. left
6. looked	20. spoke	34. lay
7. drew	21. broken	35. laid
8. reviewed	22. frozen	36. May
9. are buying	23. begun	37. raised
10. was explaining	24. drank	38. rose
11. does reveal	25. sung	39. sat
12. will decide	26. ran	40. set
13. was created	27. saw	
14. had harvested	28. taken	

HANDBOOK SECTION 6

Using Modifiers

Page 327, Exercise A

1. That (jockey), blue (shirt), satin (shirt), black (racehorse)
2. Happy (teammates), muddy (field)
3. Two (Mercedes), sleek (Mercedes), silver (Mercedes), circular (driveway)
4. comfortable (I), plaid (shirt), flannel (shirt), corduroy (jeans), brown (boots), suede (boots)
5. Mexican (belt), African (shirt), that (shop), new (shop)
6. red (leaves), orange (leaves), yellow (leaves), brown (leaves), beautiful (scene)
7. tall (player), wiry (player), free-throw (line), winning (basket)
8. Wicker (baskets), white (daisies), yellow (roses)
9. these (jeans), two (years)
10. complex (formation), grimy (envelope), old (envelope)

Page 328, Exercise B

1. red	5. full	9. smooth, easy
2. steamy, strange	6. fresh, good	10. great
3. warm	7. happy	
4. busy, noisy	8. light	

Page 331, Exercise A

1. These shelves are higher than those over there.
2. The Honda is the smallest of these three motorcycles.
3. Correct
4. It was the most awful storm I had ever seen.
5. Our new dog is much friendlier than the old one.
6. Correct
7. It was the warmest day of the summer.
8. Biology is harder than any other subject in school.
9. What happened was even more surprising.
10. The funniest thing happened yesterday.

Page 331, Exercise B

1. That was the worse of the two jokes.
2. Her joke was the best of all.
3. Correct
4. Correct
5. She had less time than usual.
6. Mine was worse, but Janet's was the worst.
7. This is the best I can do.
8. That was a better game than the one last week.
9. At the least noise Annie jumped.
10. Between reggae and disco, reggae is the harder for me to dance to.

Page 334, Exercise A

1. *hurriedly* modifies *left*, tells *how*
2. *never* modifies *have studied*, tells *to what extent*
3. *vigorously* modifies *raced*, tells *how*
4. *quite* modifies *informative*, tells *to what extent*
5. *rather* modifies *careful*, tells *to what extent*
6. *painfully* modifies *limped*, tells *how*
7. *brightly* modifies *shone*, tells *how*
8. *lazily* modifies *drifted*, tells *how*
9. *heavily* modifies *fell*, tells *how*
10. *immediately* modifies *stopped*, tells *when*

Page 335, Exercise B

1. *again* modifies *has started*, tells *when*
2. *too* modifies *late*, tells *to what extent; late* modifies *arrived*, tells *when*
3. *usually* modifies *stay*, tells *to what extent*
4. *aimlessly* modifies *wander*, tells *how*
5. *somewhat* modifies *unsure*, tells *to what extent*
6. *weakly* modifies *smiled*, tells *how*
7. *early* modifies *arrived*, tells *when*

8. *quite* modifies *smoothly,* tells *to what extent; smoothly* modifies *went,* tells *how*
9. *usually* modifies *ideal,* tells *to what extent*
10. *extremely* modifies *important,* tells *to what extent*

Page 335, Exercise C

surely	roughly	beautifully	peacefully	carefully
icily	cruelly	smoothly	dizzily	happily
fully	heavily	terribly	crazily	coolly
loudly	sadly	impatiently	grimly	hopefully

Page 337, Exercise A

1. faster, fastest
2. more wildly, most wildly
3. harder, hardest
4. more happily, most happily
5. more closely, most closely
6. longer, longest
7. more bravely, most bravely
8. more slowly, most slowly
9. more recently, most recently
10. more naturally, most naturally

Page 337, Exercise B

1. Correct
2. Vacation ended sooner than we had expected.
3. Write the directions out more completely.
4. These photographs were trimmed better than those.
5. That fish jumped higher than any other.
6. This recipe is the most consistently successful of all.
7. Can't you walk faster than that?
8. Correct
9. He tried harder than Wayne.
10. Will you read that paragraph again more slowly, please.

Page 339, Exercise A

1. *two* modifies *men; angry* modifies *men; soon* modifies *exchanged*
2. *Red, white,* and *blue* modify *bunting; decoratively* modifies *was hung*
3. *quite* modifies *promptly; promptly* modifies *paid*
4. *rather* modifies *cautiously; cautiously* modifies *answered*
5. *young* modifies *swimmers; eagerly* modifies *dove; large* modifies *pool*
6. *small* modifies *child; loudly* modifies *cried; dentist's* modifies *office*
7. *gracefully* modifies *moved; tiny* modifies *stage*
8. *American* modifies *ambassador; openly* modifies *spoke; honestly* modifies *spoke; foreign* modifies *policy*
9. *briskly* modifies *walked; long* modifies *train; yellow* modifies *train*
10. *That* modifies *restaurant; famous* modifies *restaurant; strawberry* modifies *pies*

Page 339, Exercise B

1. *exactly* (adverb) modifies *will arrive*
2. *carefully* (adverb) modifies *drives*
3. *really* (adverb) modifies *good*
4. *quickly* (adverb) modifies *reacted*
5. *clearly* (adverb) modifies *explained*
6. *cautiously* (adverb) modifies *peered*
7. *promptly* (adverb) modifies *appeared*
8. *beautifully* (adverb) modifies *fitted*
9. *quietly* (adverb) modifies *work*
10. *firmly* (adverb) modifies *spoke*

Page 341, Exercise

1. thick
2. bitter
3. calmly
4. badly
5. hysterically
6. reasonable
7. firmly
8. abruptly
9. empty
10. strange

Page 343, Exercise A

1. This
2. those
3. Those
4. those
5. that
6. This
7. Those
8. kinds
9. sorts
10. those

Page 344, Exercise B

1. well
2. good
3. well
4. good
5. well
6. well
7. well
8. good
9. good
10. well

Page 344, Exercise C

1. The girls could scarcely believe their ears.
2. Bryan has had no driving lesson this week. (*or* Bryan hasn't had any driving lesson this week.)
3. Rhoda has never been sick. (*or* Rhoda hasn't ever been sick.)
4. The movers could hardly lift the heavy box.
5. There is no time for games. (*or* There isn't any time for games.)
6. Correct
7. Ms. Ryan won't let anybody use the power tools.
8. Correct
9. Correct
10. We had plenty of Fritos, but Ellen didn't want any.

1. hilarious (joke)
2. iron (gate)
3. log (cabins)
4. rusty (truck), green (truck)
5. One (engine), old (plane)
6. comfortable (corner), current (magazines)
7. French (singer), several (notes), sour (notes)
8. That (garage), three (cars)
9. Most (students), formal (prom)
10. that (statue), Roman (statue), central (plaza)
11. happy
12. high
13. rough
14. dangerous
15. unfriendly
16. taller
17. more jealous
18. better
19. rustier
20. most difficult
21. slowly (walked)
22. patiently (fastened)
23. crisply (saluted)
24. generally (broadcasts), everywhere (broadcasts)
25. sympathetically (listened), very (sad)
26. Fortunately (were), quite (neat)
27. down (sat), noisily (talked)
28. much (cozier)
29. too (much), much (talks)
30. Yesterday (got), very (bad)
31. worse
32. more sadly
33. best
34. more firmly
35. highest
36. terrible
37. politely
38. any
39. well
40. Those, sudden

HANDBOOK SECTION 7

Using Prepositions and Conjunctions

Page 349, Exercise A

1. until tomorrow
2. up the stairs, into the room
3. with several passengers, in a cornfield
4. During the night, by thunder
5. After the play, to Mike's house
6. of Franklin Park, about the noise pollution
7. around the coach, for last-minute instructions
8. against the wall, on the shelf
9. without power, for several hours
10. In the library, on various bookshelves

Page 350, Exercise B

1. In July, to Florida, for a visit, to my grandparents
2. before school, on Friday
3. over the stadium, during the baseball game
4. on Green Bay Road
5. On the island, of Oahu
6. With a straw hat, in her hand, down the ramp
7. in the Coliseum, with a 93-yard run
8. to the top, of the John Hancock Building
9. across the lagoon, without help
10. near the expressway, around the clock

Page 350, Exercise A

1. Adverb	4. Adverb	7. Adverb	9. Adverb
2. Preposition	5. Preposition	8. Preposition	10. Adverb
3. Adverb	6. Adverb		

Page 351, Exercise B

1. Preposition	4. Preposition	7. Adverb	9. Preposition
2. Preposition	5. Adverb	8. Preposition	10. Preposition
3. Adverb	6. Preposition		

Page 354, Exercise A

1. in the navy sport coat (man)—adjective phrase
   for the Celtics (plays)—adverb phrase
2. at the bottom (sat)—adverb phrase
   of the staircase (bottom)—adjective phrase
3. through the windows (peered)—adverb phrase
   of the deserted mansion (windows)—adjective phrase
4. to her soup (added)—adverb phrase
5. in the white suit (woman)—adjective phrase
6. over the top (sign)—adjective phrase
   of the door (top)—adjective phrase
7. on the east side (window)—adjective phrase
   of the garage (side)—adjective phrase
8. near the back (performer)—adjective phrase
   of the stage (back)—adjective phrase
9. in the water (rowboat)—adjective phrase
   near the dock (water)—adjective phrase
10. in the box (are)—adverb phrase
    under the workbench (box)—adjective phrase

1. on the jet (passengers)—adjective phrase
2. above space modules (hangs)—adverb phrase
   in the museum (modules)—adejctive phrase
3. to the shop (are going)—adverb phrase
   down the street (shop)—adjective phrase
4. with a wide angle lens (took)—adverb phrase
5. on the door (sign)—adjective phrase
   in the office (door)—adjective phrase
   at 1:00 P.M. (will end)—adverb phrase
6. about astrology (article)—adjective phrase
7. on television (movie)—adjective phrase
8. for her contributions (is known)—adverb phrase
   in social work (contributions)—adjective phrase
9. about my visit (essay)—adjective phrase
   to New York (visit)—adjective phrase
10. with small children (work)—adjective phrase

1. and (*farmers* and *miners*—subject)
2. and (*rain* and *visibility*—subject)
3. Either . . . or (*staff* and *staff*—subject)
4. and (*Tom* and *I*—subject)
5. and (*breeze, temperatures,* and *skies*—subject)
6. and (*corn* and *chicken*—object)
7. or (*movies* and *rink*—object of preposition)
8. and (*Marcia* and *I*—subject), or (*game* and *meet*—object of preposition)
9. and (*slowly* and *methodically*—adverb)
10. and (*industrial* and *rural*—adjective)

1. Conjunction—and; Connected Words—farmers, miners
2. Conjunction—and; Connected Words—Freezing rain, poor visibility
3. Conjunction—Either . . . or; Connected Words—the yearbook staff, the newspaper staff
4. Conjunction—and; Connected Words—Tom, I
5. Conjunction—and; Connected Words—slight breeze, pleasant temperatures, overcast skies
6. Conjunction—and; Connected Words—corn on the cob, barbequed chicken
7. Conjunction—or; Connected Words—to the movies, to the roller rink

8. Conjunction—and; Connected Words—Marcia, I
   Conjunction—either . . . or; Connected Words—to the water polo
   game, to the indoor tennis meet
9. Conjunction—and; Connected Words—slowly, methodically
10. Conjunction—both . . . and; Connected Words—industrial, rural

Page 357, Exercise B

1. Compound subject—Neither the newspaper nor the radio
2. Compound adjective—strenuous but enjoyable
3. Compound subject—Either Earl Campbell or Franco Harris
4. Compound direct object—an opera (with Leontyne Price) or the
   Grand Kabuki (by the National Theatre of Japan)
5. Compound adverb—long and hard
6. Compound verb—stared, (then) glared, and (finally) grinned
7. Compound subject—(The) roadblock and (the) detour
8. Compound subject—Skateboards, painter's pants, Bubble Yum, and
   Frisbees
9. Compound direct object—neither avocados nor asparagus
10. Compound predicate—raised enough money for the class trip but also
    made a donation to the children's hospital.

Page 357, Exercise C   Sentences will vary.

Page 358, Review

1. on the safe
2. during this season
3. near the stadium
4. with hot sauce
5. of us, to our table
6. without a bag of rock salt
7. at the bottom, of the movie screen
8. of the race, in the newspaper
9. in the display case, by Lindsay
10. At the sound, of the gun, into the pool
11. of vitamins—Adjective
12. about the job interview—Adverb
13. by Dutch elm disease—Adverb
14. on electrified rails—Adverb
15. of the convertible—Adjective
16. on their birthdays—Adverb
17. after this one—Adjective
18. from the Big Ten—Adjective
19. on New Year's Day—Adverb
20. in the hallway—Adjective

21. Rod Stewart or Jackson Browne (compound direct object)
22. Neither Kim nor Rebecca (compound subject)
23. bright and spacious (compound predicate adjective)
24. routine but dangerous (compound adjective)
25. neither a radio nor a blanket (compound direct object)
26. both a wrestler and a boxer (compound predicate noun)
27. holidays and weekends (compound object of the preposition *On*)
28. loudly but calmly (compound adverb)
29. demanded and got (compound verb)
30. either Ms. Dean or her assistant (compound indirect object)
31. Spain and Italy (compound object of the preposition *to*)
32. The king and queen (compound subject)
33. both the house and the car (compound direct object)
34. soar and float (compound verb)
35. Congress and the nation (compound indirect object)

Review of Parts of Speech

Page 361, Exercise A

1. now—adverb
2. Many—pronoun
3. vigorous—adjective
4. quite—adverb
5. time—noun
6. six—adjective
7. use—verb
8. and—conjunction
9. In—preposition
10. Wow—interjection

Page 361, Exercise B

1. Yuck—interjection
2. for—preposition
3. staff—noun
4. Somebody—pronoun
5. too—adverb
6. or—conjunction
7. Greek—adjective
8. answered—verb
9. She—pronoun
10. in—preposition

Page 363, Exercise A

1. Which—adjective
2. Which—pronoun
3. fair—noun
4. fair—adjective
5. note—adjective
6. note—verb
7. drive—noun
8. drive—verb
9. by—preposition
10. by—adverb

Page 363, Exercise B

1. fire—verb
2. fire—noun
3. low—adverb
4. low—adjective
5. That—adjective
6. That—pronoun
7. paper—adjective
8. paper—noun
9. narrow—verb
10. narrow—adjective

Page 364, Review

1. Halt—interjection
2. customs—adjective
3. travel—noun
4. special—adjective
5. Suddenly—adverb
6. has—verb
7. this—adjective
8. tooth—adjective
9. Hurry—interjection
10. you—pronoun
11. but—preposition
12. evening—adjective
13. Aha—interjection
14. efficiently—adverb
15. Signs—noun
16. Very—adverb
17. on—preposition
18. technician—noun
19. or—conjunction
20. Which—pronoun
21. Nobody—pronoun
22. those—adjective
23. park—noun
24. nor—conjunction
25. hers—pronoun

HANDBOOK SECTION 9

Sentence Patterns

Page 366, Exercise

1. Eli teased Sarah.
2. Some athletes are people.
3. The winner is Lisa.
4. Summer follows autumn.
5. Tony passed most runners.
6. Weekdays are Mondays.

Page 367, Exercise A

N	V
1. New boots	hurt.
2. A shipment	arrived today.
3. Vacation	flew by.
4. The glass	broke.
5. Old wounds	heal slowly.
6. Jesse	swam furiously.

Page 367, Exercise B (Answers will vary.)

N	V
1. A building	collapsed.
2. Two pigeons	landed nearby.
3. The cycle	sped away.
4. Lucille	watched closely.
5. The baby pig	squealed.

Page 367, Exercise C   Answers will vary.

Page 368, Exercise A

N	V	N
1. Tony	bought	a record.
2. Dan	polished	the car.
3. My sister	trains	horses.
4. We	expected	fireworks.
5. I	finished	the yogurt.
6. Marilyn	plays	basketball.
7. Practice	makes	perfect.
8. Rodney	prepared	lunch.

Page 368, Exercise B   (Answers will vary.)

N	V	N
1. Mike	missed	the point.
2. Karen	told	our fortunes.
3. The committee	suggested	a new plan.
4. Mrs. Ford	dented	her car.
5. John Lennon	wrote	that song.
6. The store	sells	stereo equipment.

Page 368, Exercise C   Sentences will vary.

Page 369, Exercise A

N	V	N	N
1. Stamp collecting	made	me	money.
2. A portable radio	brought	us	the news.
3. Your T-shirt	gives	the world	your message.
4. Jean	told	Suzanne	the rumor.
5. We	sent	our cousins	a telegram.
6. Our team	gave	the winners	a cheer.

Page 369, Exercise B   (Answers will vary.)

N	V	N	N
	N	V	N	N
1. Terry	brought	Jerome	a lunch tray.
2. Carla	offered	Cindy	a job.
3. Everyone	gave	us	support.
4. Tim	owes	Kevin	four dollars.
5. I	sent	my friends	postcards.

Page 369, Exercise C   Sentences will vary.

Page 370, Exercise A

N	LV	N
1. Lenny	was	the cook.
2. Fruit	was	the dessert.
3. This restaurant	is	a hit.
4. The capital	is	Katmandu.
5. Alicia	is	an artist.
6. The sidewalk	is	a mess.
7. Sneakers	are	shoes.
8. A pheasant	is	a bird.

Page 370, Exercise B   (Answers will vary.)

N	LV	N
1. Monday	is	my lucky day.
2. Frank	was	co-captain.
3. Oils	are	liquids.
4. Julia	is	a bicycle racer.
5. The stars	were	decorations.

Page 370, Exercise C   Sentences will vary.

Page 371, Exercise A

N	LV	Adj
1. Charlie	seems	patient.
2. These peppers	are	hot.
3. The tomatoes	were	juicy.
4. The horses	sound	nervous.
5. Robin	felt	weary.
6. The room	was	dark.
7. The view	was	spectacular.
8. His ideas	were	excellent.

Page 371, Exercise B (Answers will vary.)

N	LV	Adj
1. Foster	looked	cheerful.
2. My pack	seems	heavy.
3. Ginny	is	alone.
4. City Hall	is	open.
5. Sue	sounded	sad.

Page 371, Exercise C Sentences will vary.

Page 372, Review (Answers will vary.)

A. 1. The general surrendered.
    2. Their bus stalled.
    3. Kim swims powerfully.

B. 1. We enjoyed the concert.
    2. Everyone ate lunch.
    3. Brian remembered the answer.

C. 1. Daniel gave his brother a book.
    2. Alison wrote the editor a letter.
    3. Everyone gave the guitarist a hand.

D. 1. That strip of land is the airfield.
    2. The violin is my favorite instrument.
    3. That hammer is a good tool.

E. 1. Samantha felt miserable.
    2. The drum solo was too long.
    3. Rhonda seemed happy.

F. Sentences will vary.

HANDBOOK SECTION 10

Using Verbals

Page 376, Exercise A

1. Skydiving (gerund, subject of *takes*)
2. Rushing (gerund, subject of *can waste*)
3. Cleaning the attic (gerund phrase, subject of *was*)
4. Washing that wall (gerund phrase, subject of *took*)

5. Painting the scenery (gerund phrase, subject of *took*)
6. Running (gerund, subject of *has become*)
7. Putting on a play (gerund phrase, subject of *takes*)
8. panelling the basement (gerund phrase, direct object of *started*)
9. pottery making (gerund phrase, object of the preposition *for*)
10. quick thinking (gerund phrase, direct object of *requires*)

Page 376, Exercise B

1. fencing (gerund, direct object of *learned*)
2. learning a new alphabet (gerund phrase, object of the preposition *by*)
3. Waiting on tables (gerund phrase, subject of *is*)
4. Visiting Dallas (gerund phrase, subject of *was*)
5. motorcycling (gerund, direct object of *has liked*)
6. Wearing sunglasses (gerund phrase, subject of *rests*)
7. overeating (gerund, object of the preposition *from*)
8. walking in the rain (gerund phrase, direct object of *likes*)
9. Eating outside (gerund phrase, subject of *was*)
10. Driving to Alaska (gerund phrase, subject of *would be*)

Page 379, Exercise A

1. exhausted (participle, modifying *runners*)
2. Moving effortlessly (participial phrase, modifying *skaters*)
3. Jumping clear (participial phrase, modifying *Nan*)
4. Crossing the old bridge (participial phrase, modifying *she*)
5. Frozen (participle, modifying *pie*)
6. Tested in our laboratories (participial phrase, modifying *parts*)
7. Spread thin (participial phrase, modifying *glue*)
8. Looking through binoculars (participial phrase, modifying *Jim*)
9. Concentrating deeply (participial phrase, modifying *center*)
10. Moving quickly (participial phrase, modifying *goalie*)

Page 379, Exercise B

1. Seeing the rain (participial phrase, modifying *Mr. Mill*)
2. Clutching the phone tightly (participial phrase, modifying *she*)
3. hitting the taillight (participial phrase, modifying *ball*)
4. Waiting patiently (participial phrase, modifying *passengers*)
5. Driving hard (participial phrase, modifying *back*); running (participle, modifying *back*)
6. worn by rare birds (participial phrase, modifying *band*)
7. leaving the quarry (participial phrase, modifying *trucks*)
8. Fascinated by the talk (participial phrase, modifying *we*)
9. lying on the table (participial phrase, modifying *paperback*)
10. Breathing hard (participial phrase, modifying *Nancy*)

Page 380, Exercise

1. Watching—gerund
2. Watching—participle
3. Fixing—gerund
4. Fixing—participle
5. Cleaning—gerund
6. Cleaning—participle
7. Removing—gerund
8. Panning—participle
9. Moving—participle
10. Swimming—gerund

Page 384, Exercise A

1. to watch "Saturday Night Live" (infinitive phrase, direct object of *plan*)
2. to explain the new procedures (infinitive phrase, direct object of *wants*)
3. To finish this project by Monday (infinitive phrase, subject of *is*)
4. to remember the address (infinitive phrase, direct object of *tried*)
5. to see the Mets' game (infinitive phrase, modifying *late*)
6. to bring our registration cards to orientation (infinitive phrase, direct object of *were told*)
7. to encourage the Cowboys (infinitive phrase, direct object of *tried*)
8. to use (infinitive, modifying *book*)
9. to get a flashlight (infinitive phrase, modifying *ran*)
10. to do (infinitive, modifying *homework*)

Page 384, Exercise B

1. to climb (infinitive, modifying *steep*)
2. to do (infinitive, modifying *thing*); to wait (infinitive, predicate noun)
3. to eat breakfast at the pancake house (infinitive phrase, direct object of *Would like*)
4. To read the first two chapters of this book (infinitive phrase, subject of *is*)
5. to help her to finish the job (infinitive phrase, modifying *someone*); to finish the job (infinitive phrase, modifying *help*)
6. to get a driver's permit (infinitive phrase, modifying *young*)
7. to get a job in Alaska (infinitive phrase, direct object of *wanted*)
8. to buy film (infinitive phrase, direct object of *Did remember*)
9. to fill the tank with unleaded gas (infinitive phrase, direct object of *Remind*)
10. to play hockey after school (infinitive phrase, direct object of *Do want*)

Page 386, Exercise A

1. to catch a glimpse of John Travolta—infinitive
2. Accepting praise—gerund
3. to finish furniture—infinitive

4. Using bottles and crayons—participle
5. picking—gerund
6. to race him—infinitive
7. Waking up—gerund
8. to swallow—infinitive
9. broken—participle
10. Resigning her job—participle

Page 386, Exercise B

1. developing film—gerund
2. to call—infinitive
3. to create a new image—infinitive
4. badly beaten—participle
5. learning—participle
6. Falling asleep in class—gerund
7. Grinning widely—participle
8. judging the contest—participle
9. passing accurately—gerund
10. to see that exhibit—infinitive

Page 387, Review

1. Kidnapping
2. applauding loudly
3. advertising on children's TV
4. Replacing the muffler
5. persuading people
6. broken
7. Lying in a hammock
8. Sighting the strange lights
9. Dressed for a ballgame
10. using a compass
11. to ridicule
12. to win back the title
13. to tape her favorite albums
14. to beat
15. to drive a stick shift
16. returning—Participle
17. biking around the lake—Gerund
18. deceived by the con man—Participle
19. winning friends with gifts—Gerund
20. to explore Brazil—Infinitive

Making Subjects and Verbs Agree

Page 390, Exercise A

1. is
2. looks
3. are
4. were
5. arrives
6. is
7. was
8. have
9. were
10. has

Page 390, Exercise B

1. is
2. were
3. is
4. contributes
5. belong
6. was
7. report
8. coach
9. like
10. require

Page 391, Exercise A

1. haven't
2. call
3. are
4. have
5. report
6. arrive
7. dock
8. are
9. needs
10. are

Page 391, Exercise B

1. is
2. tastes
3. look
4. have
5. obscure
6. is
7. help
8. tune
9. wakens
10. publicize

Page 393, Exercise A

1. comes
2. were
3. needs
4. is
5. earn
6. expects
7. compares
8. was
9. have
10. plays

Page 393, Exercise B

1. uses
2. is
3. shows
4. go
5. is
6. dries
7. was
8. are
9. practice
10. is

Page 394, Exercise A

1. doesn't
2. is
3. are
4. goes
5. doesn't
6. are
7. is
8. doesn't
9. are
10. are

Page 395, Exercise B

1. comes
2. Doesn't
3. is
4. doesn't
5. are
6. were
7. do
8. are
9. is
10. are

Page 396, Review

1. change
2. is
3. cause
4. have
5. circles
6. looks
7. run
8. costs
9. has
10. employ
11. is
12. have
13. keeps
14. wears
15. has
16. is
17. read
18. have
19. are
20. doesn't
21. doesn't
22. doesn't
23. are
24. is
25. are

Using Compound and Complex Sentences

Page 399, Exercise A

1. Movie-goers in the 1920's | admired such greats as Greta Garbo, Rudolph Valentino, and Douglas Fairbanks.
2. Slapstick comedy | was performed by Charlie Chaplin, Harold Lloyd, and Buster Keaton.
3. "Talkies," or movies with sound, | became popular in the late 1920's.
4. The movies in the 1930's | starred such people as Shirley Temple, Mae West, and Clark Gable.
5. The city of Hollywood | was known as "the celluloid paradise."
6. One of the greatest movies | was released in 1939.
7. This particular movie | was discussed by hundreds of magazines and newspapers.
8. *Gone with the Wind* | swept movie-goers off their feet.
9. The stars, Vivien Leigh and Clark Gable, | were recognized by everyone.
10. Their movie | became a film classic.

Page 399, Exercise B

1. teens and youth (compound subject)
2. Mini-skirts, long hair, Afros, and Beatlemania (compound subject)
3. have danced and have listened (compound verb)
4. bands and music (compound subject); 1940's and 1950's (compound direct object)
5. skateboards, platform shoes, Levis, Adidas, and T-shirts (compound direct object)
6. albums and tapes (compound direct object)
7. music and fashion (compound subject)
8. The Beatles and the Rolling Stones (compound subject)
9. radios and stereos (compound subject); Jimi Hendrix, Linda Ronstadt, Diana Ross, Amazing Grace, and many others (compound object of preposition)
10. you and your friends (compound subject)

Page 402, Exercise A

Subject/Verb	Conjunction	Subject/Verb
1. You must follow	or	you will miss
2. Craig dislikes	but	he does like
3. Sandy wanted	but	boss would allow
4. I will ride	but	I need
5. It rained	and	game was cancelled

Subject/Verb	Conjunction	Subject/Verb
6. we played	and	we had
7. Amanda spoke	but	no one could hear
8. rate had risen	but	cost had gone
9. you Will sell	or	you will trade
10. missile disintegrated	and	parts landed

Page 402, Exercise B

Subject/Verb	Conjunction	Subject/Verb
1. game was scheduled	but	speech pre-empted
2. Lucinda, I went	and	brothers did
3. you Do like	or	you do prefer
4. Amelia Earhart was	but	she became
5. Tanya, I were playing	but	I like
6. Babe Ruth was	but	Babe Didrikson contributed
7. I enjoy	but	*My Darling, My Hamburger* is
8. lake froze	and	fishermen set
9. Ted entered	and	guests yelled
10. women change	but	others keep

Page 404, Exercise A

1. Compound Sentence
2. Compound Sentence
3. Simple Sentence
4. Simple Sentence
5. Compound Sentence
6. Compound Sentence
7. Compound Sentence
8. Simple Sentence
9. Simple Sentence
10. Simple Sentence

Page 404, Exercise B

1. Simple Sentence
2. Simple Sentence
3. Simple Sentence
4. Compound Sentence
5. Simple Sentence
6. Compound Sentence
7. Simple Sentence
8. Simple Sentence
9. Simple Sentence
10. Compound Sentence

Page 406, Exercise A

1. started, but
2. Eve, and
3. Correct
4. Correct
5. work, or
6. Correct
7. Tyson, and
8. rope, and
9. Correct
10. jockey, but

Page 407, Exercise B

1. villages, and
2. homework, but
3. Correct
4. Correct
5. Correct
6. happenings, and
7. Correct
8. Correct
9. name, or
10. escalator, but

Page 410, Exercise (Sentences will vary.)

1. because it was very foggy
2. since the window is broken
3. when the car stopped
4. when the dog howled
5. when the power went off
6. if you can go
7. when our packages are ready
8. after the party ended
9. after the crowd had left
10. because it rained on Saturday

Page 410, Exercise A

1. <u>that</u> <u>has</u> double layers of ingredients
2. why <u>Sarah</u> <u>seems</u> unhappy
3. when <u>you</u> <u>come</u> back
4. so that <u>I</u> <u>wouldn't forget</u> them
5. when <u>I</u> <u>called</u> for you
6. than <u>I</u> <u>thought</u>
7. although <u>she</u> usually <u>knows</u> the answers
8. While <u>we</u> <u>were</u> in Philadelphia
9. Although the <u>land</u> around Denver <u>is</u> flat
10. until the <u>field</u> <u>is</u> drier

Page 411, Exercise B

1. because a <u>drought</u> <u>had cut</u> the supply
2. where deep-dish <u>pizza</u> <u>was developed</u>
3. that <u>Teresa</u> <u>drives</u> too fast
4. after <u>he</u> <u>had talked</u> to his girlfriend
5. if <u>she</u> <u>would work</u> on Tuesday
6. because <u>he</u> <u>works</u> at night
7. When <u>business</u> <u>slows</u> down
8. where the <u>astronauts</u> <u>train</u>
9. as <u>we</u> <u>fell</u> into the pool
10. that <u>she</u> <u>is</u> not a good loser

Page 412, Exercise A

1. When <u>we</u> <u>arrived</u> in Seattle
2. Before <u>we</u> <u>could visit</u> the small villages
3. because <u>we</u> <u>had saved</u> it from Christmas
4. Since <u>it</u> <u>began</u> to rain
5. as <u>we</u> <u>approached</u>
6. As the <u>mist</u> <u>cleared</u>
7. If South American mail <u>planes</u> <u>are</u> late
8. before <u>we</u> <u>left</u>
9. Although <u>he</u> <u>had lived</u> all his life in England
10. If <u>you</u> <u>had been</u> there on Saturday

Page 413, Exercise B

1. If <u>you</u> <u>want</u> to stop
2. When the <u>light</u> <u>goes</u> on
3. If <u>negotiations</u> <u>succeed</u>
4. as long as <u>you</u> <u>exercise</u>
5. because <u>all</u> of the motels <u>were</u> full
6. Although <u>he</u> <u>consulted</u> with advisers
7. when <u>she</u> <u>was</u> six
8. Whenever the <u>actor</u> <u>went</u> to New York
9. unless patrol <u>cars</u> <u>are</u> nearby
10. until <u>Roberto</u> <u>arrives</u>

Page 416, Exercise A

1. family—<u>who</u> <u>owns</u> the grocery
2. Burt—<u>who</u> <u>was</u> still awake
3. woman—<u>who</u> <u>teaches</u> at the college
4. team—<u>that</u> <u>wins</u> this game
5. anyone—<u>who</u> <u>had seen</u> the accident
6. woman—<u>who</u> <u>was carrying</u> many packages
7. picture—<u>that</u> <u>you</u> <u>gave</u> us
8. days—<u>when</u> <u>everything</u> <u>went</u> wrong
9. coat—<u>that</u> <u>you</u> <u>want</u>
10. doctor—with whom <u>we</u> <u>consulted</u>

Page 416, Exercise B

1. team—<u>that has won</u> the Stanley Cup
2. issues—<u>that concerned</u> the people
3. games—<u>that are</u> most popular
4. time—when <u>I was</u> afraid
5. relatives—whom <u>Ernie visited</u>
6. Kentucky Derby—<u>which is held</u> at Churchill Downs
7. book—that <u>I was telling</u> you about
8. factory—where <u>candy is made</u>
9. Summerfest—<u>which is held</u> in August
10. place—where <u>we can talk</u>

Page 419, Exercise A

1. whatever <u>you decide</u> (direct object)
2. <u>Whoever wins</u> (subject)
3. <u>who told</u> you that (direct object)
4. where the <u>Marcuses live</u> (direct object)
5. <u>Whoever appeared</u> (subject)
6. what <u>you said</u> (object of preposition)
7. <u>whoever is</u> at the door (object of preposition)
8. where <u>Kevin was going</u> (direct object)
9. whatever <u>candidate is chosen</u> (direct object)
10. How the <u>project will be funded</u> (subject)

Page 419, Exercise B

1. what <u>I had expected</u> (predicate noun)
2. that our <u>car was fine</u> (direct object)
3. where <u>she had left</u> her books (direct object)
4. whatever <u>Rob did</u> (direct object)
5. <u>Whoever sees</u> a fire (subject)
6. Whatever <u>Jerry cooks</u> (subject)
7. how <u>she reads</u> palms (direct object)
8. what <u>we get</u> (object of preposition)
9. What an <u>accountant does</u> (subject)
10. that the <u>day went</u> quickly (direct object)

Page 420, Exercise A

1. when Dr. Jordan was speaking (adverb clause, modifying *arrived*)
2. that we agreed on (adjective clause, modifying *time*)
3. while the TV is on (adverb clause, modifying *Can study*)
4. who the man was (noun clause, direct object)
5. before the snowball hit him (adverb clause, modifying *ducked*)
6. that leaves at 7:00 P.M. (adjective clause, modifying *plane*)
7. that the experiment is possible (noun clause, direct object)
8. that we would have a holiday tomorrow (noun clause, direct object)
9. when he was growing up (adverb clause, modifying *lived*)
10. How the engine works (noun clause, subject)

Page 421, Exercise B

1. that are not rational (adjective clause, modifying *beliefs*)
2. when people fear the unknown (adverb clause, modifying *begin*)
3. even though they started long ago (adverb clause, modifying *exist*)
4. how various superstitions began (noun clause, direct object)
5. that black cats bring bad luck (adjective clause, modifying *superstition*)
6. that a cat was a witch in disguise (noun clause, direct object)
7. that is based on superstition (adjective clause, modifying *practice*)
8. When people sneeze (adverb clause, modifying *say*)
9. that breath was life (noun clause, direct object)
10. because breath was lost (adverb clause, modifying *was feared*)

Page 422, Exercise A (Answers will vary.)

1. S—After the argument we shook hands.
2. F—After the show had ended, everyone applauded.
3. F—The art fair was held where the school always has its football games.
4. S—Where is the box of candy?
5. S—Since yesterday morning the air has been clear.
6. F—Since we have no food left, we must hike back to town.
7. S—Because of the storm our lights went off.
8. F—I stayed in bed because the doctor advised plenty of rest.
9. S—When are you leaving for Dallas?
10. F—When the old mine was closed down, many people left town.

Page 422, Exercise B (Answers will vary.)

1. S—Down the mountain rolled a boulder.
2. F—I have missed the bus every day since the beginning of school.
3. S—Since you agree, we can go ahead with the plans.
4. F—The shouting continued until the manager came out and stopped the noise.

5. F—This is the spot where the car went off the road.
6. S—When the wind is from the south, we get rain.
7. S—Where is the box for this puzzle?
8. F—Before the lifeguard could reach the boat, it capsized.
9. F—We talked while we waited for our ride.
10. S—Although the movie was cancelled, we had a group discussion.

Page 424, Exercise A

1. Simple	4. Complex	7. Simple	9. Complex
2. Compound	5. Complex	8. Compound	10. Complex
3. Simple	6. Simple		

Page 424, Exercise B

1. Compound	4. Simple	7. Simple	9. Compound
2. Simple	5. Complex	8. Complex	10. Complex
3. Complex	6. Compound		

Page 425, Review

	Subjects	Verbs
1.	landlord	raised
2.	Virgil and Eric	are paddling
3.	Van	wrote and got
4.	Samantha	put and went
5.	Dr. Early	checked and prescribed

6. Carrie dreams each night, but she never remembers her dreams.
7. Betsy headed for the beach, and the dogs followed.
8. The city took bids for highway construction, and Quinlan got the contract.
9. Tom is based in Chicago, but most of his work is in the suburbs.
10. This theater has an unusual policy; it books only PG-rated movies.
11. The flag went down and a penalty was called.
12. Several players can place-kick, but only Dara is accurate.
13. The manager asked the youths for identification, and they quickly left.
14. Most of the footage was destroyed, but some of the film was salvaged.
15. Japanese women sometimes wear kimonos; Indian women often wear saris.
16. The goalie dove, but the puck slid by.
17. Someone flipped a switch, and the street lit up.
18. Those laws are out-of-date, but they are still on the books.
19. I read my horoscope, and it predicted sudden wealth.

20. The starlet desperately wanted publicity, and she got it.
21. that I want
22. that the defense was tiring
23. because he wanted to look older
24. how the floodlight worked
25. when it sat out in the rain
26. when he was in the Marines
27. that all look alike
28. who is an author and a poet
29. that the job would be easy
30. Unless the Cubs bounce back
31. that the bus driver takes only exact change
32. before she started her job
33. who worked at the factory
34. what you are thinking
35. that the game had been rigged
36. Complex
37. Compound
38. Simple
39. Complex
40. Compound

HANDBOOK SECTION 13

Capitalization

Page 429, Exercise A
 1. I told my mother that I had a doctor's appointment.
 2. She said, "Please ask Dr. Hernandez to call me."
 3. The new teacher is from Paris, France.
 4. He is a Parisian.
 5. Would you tell Mom I'll be a little late for dinner?
 6. The first book of the Bible is the Book of Genesis.
 7. My mother asked Aunt Rose if Tad and Maria could stay for lunch.
 8. Please take this message to the principal, Lynn.
 9. She says that Ms. Holchak is not in her office.
10. Some names for God are Jehovah, the Lord, and the Almighty.

Page 430, Exercise B

1. There are seven cities named Springfield.
2. The largest is in Massachusetts.
3. Our government is sometimes called a Jeffersonian democracy.
4. The new student is Toshio Kitagawa. His sister is Mieko.
5. Both of them were born in Japan.
6. Which Cairo do you mean?
7. Is it the one in Egypt or the one in Illinois?
8. Speakers were Mrs. J. P. Perez, and Ms. P. D. Cardelo.
9. All of my aunts and uncles live in California.
10. It was Captain Sherman who gave Sue and Ted the booklets on bicycle safety.

Page 431, Exercise A

1. Independence, Missouri
2. Fort Kearney, Nebraska
3. North Platte River, Fort Laramie
4. Rocky Mountains, South Pass, Wyoming
5. Rockies
6. Oregon Trail, Pacific Northwest
7. Mormon Trail, Salt Lake City, Utah
8. Great Basin, Nevada, Utah
9. Sierra Nevada Mountains, Donner Pass
10. American

Page 432, Exercise B

1. Trans-Canada Highway, Canada
2. Asia, Africa
3. Eighth Congressional District
4. Morton Township
5. Capri, Bay of Naples
6. Blue Grotto, Capri
7. Baikal
8. Siberia, Soviet Union
9. Lincoln Park Zoo
10. Gulf of Mexico, New Orleans, Memphis

Page 434, Exercise A

1. American Motors Corporation
2. Ford Pinto, Ford Fairmont
3. Pulaski High School
4. Ancient History I, Business Math II, English
5. Treaty of Paris, Spanish-American War
6. Fourth of July, American

7. Declaration of Independence, July
8. none
9. Atlantic Ocean, Amelia Earhart
10. B. C., Julius Caesar

Page 434, Exercise B

1. Hispaniola, A.D.
2. Muhammad, Islam
3. Moslems, Muslims
4. *U.S.S. Constitution*, "*Old Ironsides*"
5. *Broadway Limited*, New York, Chicago
6. Brookston Hospital, Dr. Margaret Allen
7. Munich, Germany
8. St. Luke's Hospital
9. Spanish, Russian, French, German
10. Russian, U.C.L.A.

Page 437, Exercise A

1. The, Sherlock Holmes, *Valley of Fear*, "Danger"
2. Helen Reddy, "Midnight Special"
3. The, Will Rogers, All, I, I
4. I. American
      A. The
          1. Battle of Bunker Hill
5. Don't, I
6. For, I, *Seventeen*
7. The, *Herald Tribune*
8. Very
9. Hurry, Father, If
10. We, *North Dallas Forty*

Page 437, Exercise B

1. Dear Ms. Weiss
2. "The Death of the Hired Man"
3. I. Business
      A. Correct
          1. Heading
4. *Sports Illustrated*
5. He, Such, To, But
6. "Images of Youth Past," *Life*
7. She, Has
8. I'm, We're
9. I, *The Wizard of Oz*, I, *The Wiz*
10. I, *The Song of Solomon*, Toni Morrison's

1. The umpire threatened to oust Don Baylor from the game.
2. That legislation was sponsored by Senator Jacob Javits.
3. After the Beatles broke up, George Harrison sang solo.
4. The President relaxed at Camp David in Maryland.
5. The head juror, Mr. Vernon Wills, announced the verdict to Judge Sandra Sims.
6. My mother and I have tickets to the game between the Cincinnati Reds and the Houston Astros.
7. Last Sunday Reverend Brown read from the Gospel of Luke.
8. An American Airlines jet took off for Athens, Greece, but had to land in Rome, Italy.
9. To get to Adler Planetarium, go south on Lake Shore Drive.
10. Many Easterners visit New York to see the Catskill Mountains.
11. The National Aeronautics and Space Administration is located in Houston.
12. Ascension Island is in the middle of the Atlantic Ocean.
13. "The Catbird Seat" is written by the author of "The Secret Life of Walter Mitty."
14. Chuck read *People* magazine in the waiting room of the clinic.
15. Veteran's Day, November 11, is the day we honor soldiers who fought for this country.
16. Dad asked, "Will you stop at the newsstand and get *The New York Times?*
17. A kidnapped American was found in the Venezuelan jungle.
18. On April 8, 1974, Hank Aaron hit his 715th home run.
19. Many European schools teach English.
20. Are you taking an algebra course or Business Math 300?

HANDBOOK SECTION 14

Punctuation

Page 443, Exercise A

1. Where did I put my new sweater?
2. Wow! That was quite a football game!
3. What is Dr. Harrigan's phone number?
4. Where is Sgt. Leslie's office located?
5. Help! I can't get this door open!
6. I was supposed to meet Tom at 10:30 A.M.
7. Dr. James Coogan, Jr. is going to talk about lifesaving.

8. Mary, look out!
9. Our art supplies will cost less than ten dollars, but they'll be more than $8.25.
10. My appointment with Dr. Wagner is at 11:15 A.M. on Friday.

Page 443, Exercise B

1. Dr. Elizabeth McMinn is our school principal.
2. Please send your requests to Franklin's, Ltd., P.O. Box 552, New York, N.Y.
3. While in Washington, D.C., where did you stay?
4. One mile is equal to 1.6 kilometers.
5. Luis asked if he could help me with my homework.
6. I have two broadcast bands on my radio: AM and FM.
7. UNICEF is the children's organization of the UN.
8. My parents were born in Buffalo, N.Y.
9. Rev. James M. Butler, Jr. will be the guest speaker.
10. Will you mail these coupons to the Clark Company, Inc., 301 E. Walton Place, Chicago, Illinois 60611?

Page 444, Exercise A

1. A northerly wind swept the wet, thick snow against the front door.
2. That green TR7 has worn tires, brakes, and shocks.
3. Red, white, and blue bunting decorated the speaker's stand.
4. We went to the store and bought Fritos, potato chips, pretzels, and Coke.
5. The race car skidded, did a complete turn-around, and blew out its right front tire.
6. At the movies, I like fresh, salty, buttery popcorn.
7. Strong, gusty winds blew across the lake.
8. My sister can play the guitar, the banjo, and the mandolin.
9. In order to finish the scenery, do the following: first, nail the supports together; second, paint the backdrop; and third, put away all unnecessary tools and paint.
10. Sue finished her homework, made a telephone call, and went to bed.

Page 445, Exercise B

1. The committee discussed, debated, and accepted the proposal.
2. The baffled, worn-out mail carrier slumped on our porch swing.
3. A small rabbit scooted across our doorstep, through the evergreens, and under our back porch.
4. Wool, silk, and cotton are natural cloths.
5. Bowling, skating, and running are my favorite activities.
6. A long, sleek, black limousine pulled up in front of the bank.
7. James, Joan, and Greg helped design the posters.

8. We need crepe paper, balloons, and tape to decorate the gym.
9. The speaker stated the hard, clear facts.
10. The salesclerk pulled a green scarf off the shelf, spread it flat on the counter, and told us the price.

Page 446, Exercise A

1. No, I don't think the library is open on Sundays.
2. After circling the airport for an hour, we finally landed.
3. Although the game was postponed until Friday, we had practice every morning.
4. Yes, I have finished the dishes.
5. The exam, however, will be given as scheduled.
6. Ms. Cassini, to tell the truth, was quite pleased with our panel discussion.
7. Since the Hawks lost their last ten games, they will not be in the play-offs.
8. The results of the student survey, however, will not be revealed until next week.
9. No, the mail has not been delivered.
10. Even though we arrived early, we still didn't get good seats for the basketball game.

Page 447, Exercise B

1. After we went on the hayride, we had a barbecue and played volleyball.
2. Yes, the garage has been cleaned out.
3. The game, consequently, was postponed.
4. The latest weather report, however, has predicted rain.
5. Although the heavy snow tied up the morning traffic, most companies and businesses were open as usual.
6. Yes, the intramural track meet is tomorrow.
7. Since Mardi Gras is such a celebrated occasion in New Orleans, most schools there take a holiday.
8. It is doubtful, however, that the weather will change our plans.
9. No, the garage sale isn't until next week.
10. If you look carefully at these old advertisements, you will see how different dress and housing used to be.

Page 449, Exercise A

1. "Cheerleading tryouts will be held tonight," began the announcement, "and all students are invited to take part."
2. The team captain, the player in the blue jersey, is a good student.
3. I read *Roots*, but I preferred the television series.

4. I enjoy reading science fiction novels, but I also enjoy reading mysteries.
5. She ran down the stairs and raced down the sidewalk.
6. Ms. Leoni, our new science teacher, was born in Italy.
7. Sir Georg Solti, the famous conductor, directs the Chicago Symphony Orchestra.
8. When you are finished, Kurt, will you help with this project?
9. Maria finished her supper and then went to play rehearsal.
10. John Hancock, one of the signers of the Declaration of Independence, was from Massachusetts.

Page 450, Exercise B

1. The governor's aide, Deputy Chief Roseanna Ruhl, visited Latin America.
2. Linda showed me her present, a cassette tape recorder.
3. I will wash the car, but I don't have time to wax it.
4. I asked Ms. Wright, our science teacher, about lasers.
5. Andres Segovia, the classical guitarist, will play at Orchestra Hall in May.
6. Will you come with me, or would you rather stay here?
7. Ms. Watkins, our P.E. teacher, was a member of the U.S. Olympic swim team.
8. We saw the end of the special, and then we watched the "ABC Movie of the Week."
9. "Please take the dog for a walk," said Dad.
10. Pam, this is my brother Paul.

Page 451, Exercise A

1. The bombing of Pearl Harbor on December 7, 1941, marked the beginning of World War II for the United States.
2. On August 14, 1945, Japan surrendered to the Allies.
3. The stock market crash on October 29, 1929, marked the beginning of the Great Depression.
4. Whatever you do, do it well.
5. Send your requests to Mr. R. Joseph Laya, 180 North Capitol Avenue, Denver, Colorado 80202.
6. The first state, Delaware, entered the Union on December 7, 1787.
7. The first Transcontinental Railroad was completed on May 10, 1869, in Promontory, Utah.
8. In 1874, Joseph Glidden invented barbed wire.
9. Whatever happens, happens.
10. George Washington was inaugurated in New York City on April 30, 1789, at Federal Hall.

Page 452, Exercise B

1. Because my parents work for the government, I have lived in Fairbanks, Alaska, and Madrid, Spain.
2. The Lewis and Clark expedition began on May 14, 1804, in St. Louis, Missouri, and returned there on September 23, 1806.
3. John H. Glenn, Jr. became the first American to orbit the earth on February 20, 1962, aboard the *Friendship 7*.
4. We ordered our uniforms from the J. C. Wood Company, P. O. Box 5835, Richmond, Virginia 23220.
5. Whatever it is, it is strange-looking.
6. The flight will visit Helsinki, Finland, and Stockholm, Sweden.
7. My sister was born in Tokyo, Japan, on January 1, 1965, and I was born in Frankfurt, Germany, on January 1, 1968.
8. On August 26, 1920, the amendment that gave women the right to vote was adopted.
9. The Great Chicago Fire of 1871 supposedly started in the barn at Mrs. O'Leary's, 558 DeKoven Street, Chicago, Illinois.
10. Dear Jill,

    Would you please send me the Harrisons' new address? I'd appreciate it.

    Your friend,
    Tom

Page 454, Exercise A

1. dinner; Brian
2. others; however
3. California; Dallas
   Texas; and
4. day; moreover
5. laundry; Jenny
   yard; Joan
6. Africa; a tiger
   India; a snow
   Tibet; and
7. tomorrow: your
8. between 8:30 and 8:45 A.M.
9. Madam:
   This
10. day; however

Page 454, Exercise B

1. home: a gallon
2. mystery; Sandy
3. time; nevertheless
   by 5:30
4. at 6:55 P.M.; Dad's
   at 7:15 P.M.
5. test; yet
6. sales; the
7. at 7:15 A.M.; my
   until 8:30 A.M.
8. blinding; however
   at 8:15 A.M.
9. run; and
10. Monday: tracing

Page 456, Exercise

1. up-to-date	9. sixty-two
2. twenty-six	10. sixty-eight
3. half-cut	11. great-grandparents
4. Twenty-five	12. well-to-do
5. Ninety-three	13. Thirty-two
6. three-fourths	14. twenty-first
7. twenty-three, fifty-six	15. Commander-in-Chief
8. ninety-fifth	

Page 458, Exercise A

1. We've heard that there won't be an assembly until next week.
2. Beatrix Potter's most famous work is *Peter Rabbit.*
3. Her writings and illustrations are well known in children's literature.
4. Billie Holiday's life and music were portrayed in the movie *Lady Sings the Blues.*
5. Diana Ross's performance as the jazz musician earned her an Oscar nomination.
6. Soichiro Honda's company has been producing motorcycles and cars in Japan since the 1940's.
7. I've always liked the silent movies of Mary Pickford and Charlie Chaplin.
8. All of the teachers' meetings are held in the library.
9. Babe Didrikson Zaharias's autobiography reveals her intense love for athletics and her zest for life.
10. *The Miracle Worker* is a play about Helen Keller's childhood and Annie Sullivan's efforts to help the blind and deaf Helen.

Page 458, Exercise B

1. The *1*'s and *7*'s in this ledger are difficult to tell apart.
2. The graduating classes of '79 and '80 are buying a new digital scoreboard.
3. Although she was the first woman to go into space, Valentina Tereshkova's name is not well known.
4. We've heard Beverly Sills's performance at the opera.
5. Someone's moped is parked in the Burton's driveway.
6. Isn't the girls' gymnastics meet on Saturday?
7. Clara Barton's dedication in a volunteer nurse corps led to her founding of the American Red Cross.
8. S. E. Hinton's novel, *That Was Then, This Is Now,* is one of the best books we've read this year.
9. Jenny's sister and Paula's brother are both interns at St. Mary's Hospital.
10. Nurses' training programs are thorough and demanding.

Page 460, Exercise

1. "Watch out for broken glass," he said.
   He said, "Watch out for broken glass."
   "Watch out," he said, "for broken glass."
2. "I'm sure that I am right," she said.
   She said, "I'm sure that I am right."
   "I'm sure," she said, "that I am right."
3. "Of course you're invited," I said.
   I said, "Of course you're invited."
   "Of course," I said, "you're invited."
4. "On Monday summer vacation begins," he said.
   He said, "On Monday summer vacation begins."
   "On Monday," he said, "summer vacation begins."
5. "Did you know that a jaeger is a bird?" she asked.
   She asked, "Did you know that a jaeger is a bird?"
   "Did you know," she asked, "that a jaeger is a bird?"

Page 461, Exercise A

1. "Jeff, have you seen that movie?" asked Debbie.
2. "The best part," she added, "is the ending."
3. Nicole said that I deserve better treatment.
4. "Have the committee members arrived yet?" asked Marka.
5. "Would you mind," asked Doug, "if I borrowed your jacket?"
6. Did the teacher say, "We'll meet in the gym"?
7. The speaker said that inflation must be stopped.
8. "That's the game!" yelled the announcer. "The Yanks have won!"
9. The receptionist asked us what we wanted.
10. "I never heard of such a thing," said my mother quietly. "Are you sure that is what he said?"

Page 462, Exercise B   (Answers will vary.)

1. Karen said, "Watch me while I hop this fence."
2. "I will drive you all the way home," David said.
3. Mom asked, "Are you curious about your new teacher?"
4. "Every day I check the mail," Sandy said.
5. "I like that shirt," Sarah said, "but I can't afford it."
6. The coach said, "Behind every good athlete is a lot of training."
7. "Next week," Lynn said, "I will turn sixteen."
8. "When did you begin studying English?" I asked.
9. One fan shouted, "You can do it!"
10. "Will you join us for lunch?" asked one of the girls.

Page 462, Exercise C

"What is your biggest fault?" Cecily asked, hoping to start a good discussion.

"I don't have any faults," joked Brian.

"Come on, everybody," Karen said. "Answer her question."

Steve thought a minute and finally said, "I'm too quick-tempered. I get angry much too easily."

"My biggest fault," Gloria said, "is that I'm selfish and don't consider other people enough."

Quietly, Chris added, "My big fault is that I'm terribly lazy."

"Yes," Brian said with a big grin, "I agree totally with what all of you have said."

"And your main fault," Cecily said, "is that you're much too kind."

Page 463, Exercise A

1. I liked the story "The Monkey's Paw."
2. For my poetry assignment, I read "Ex-Basketball Player."
3. Read the first chapter, "Discovery in the New World," for tomorrow.
4. The television program "Family" deals with problems and pleasures of everyday life.
5. Some of James Thurber's stories are "The Very Proper Gander," "The Shrike and the Chipmunks," and "The Unicorn in the Garden."
6. Our band played music from *Grease* and the theme from *Star Wars*.
7. The Charlie Chaplin movie *The Gold Rush* and Harold Lloyd's film *Safety Last* are two well-known silent comedies.
8. Did you see the movie *One on One?*
9. Read Chapter 2, "How We Came to the River."
10. Judy Bass's painting *Jump out of Darkness* is on display.

Page 464, Exercise B

1. "God Save the Queen" and "America" have the same melody.
2. Two of Jack's favorite programs are "Sixty Minutes" and "M*A*S*H."
3. We read the novel *The Call of the Wild* and the short story "Brown Wolf" by Jack London.
4. *Adjo Means Good-Bye* by Carrie A. Young is a story of friendship.
5. My essay entitled "Youth Today" won an honorable mention in the poetry and prose contest.
6. *One Flew Over the Cuckoo's Nest* won the Academy Award for the best picture in 1975.
7. "Old Man River" is a song from the musical *Showboat*.

8. Last week's editorial was entitled "The Mess in City Government—What Are *You* Doing about It?"
9. Barry Manilow, who has recorded such songs as "I Write the Songs" and "Dancin' in the Streets," has also written many popular advertising slogans and jingles.
10. My favorite poem is "The Revolt of the Machines" by Stephen Vincent Benet.

Page 465, Review

1. Greg asked if the hamburgers, fries, and shakes were ready.
2. Make my appointment with Dr. Stern at 3:00 P.M.
3. How right you are!
4. In addition, you have a terrific sense of humor, Carmella.
5. Delia, of course, will take the photographs.
6. Did you meet Earl Warren, Jr., the U. S. Supreme Court justice?
7. "Small incidents cause big conflicts, and the result is sometimes war," our history teacher said.
8. On Monday, April 15, 1912, the *Titanic* sank.
9. Visit the auto manufacturing plants in Detroit, Michigan.
10. My new address, one which is easy to remember, is 123 Fourth Street, Cleveland, Ohio.
11. My great-grandfather turned ninety-two last week; he was married the next day.
12. TV, radio, newspapers, and magazines reach the masses of people; therefore, they are called mass media.
13. Undoubtedly the fire broke out in the kitchen; then it spread to the dining room, living room, and bedroom.
14. The hard-working wrestling squad works out from 3:30 until 5:00 each day.
15. The following tools are used in carpentry: saws, hammers, drills, planes, and levels.
16. We collected everyone's donations to the children's hospital.
17. "Vanessa's name is spelled with one *n* and two *s*'s," said Karen.
18. "The two owners' goal," Valerie said, "is to expand the store."
19. A harsh voice yelled, "Get out!"
20. "Don't you wonder," Carla asked, "who's on the phone?"
21. "Hasn't the telephone company been here yet?" Julie asked. "The storm knocked down our wires."
22. There was a movie called *The Summer of '42*, and it had a sequel called *The Class of '44*.
23. Carlos's essay is titled "Losers I Have Known."
24. Our teacher assigned the tenth chapter, "Credit Buying," in *The Modern Consumer*.
25. The TV series "The Jeffersons" is a spin-off from "All in the Family."

Spelling

Page 469, Exercise A

1. driving
2. immobilized
3. unnecessarily
4. misspellings, writing, unacceptable
5. argument
6. believing
7. noisy
8. (none)
9. Hitchhiking, illegal
10. reemphasized, irregular

Page 470, Exercise B

1. hiking
2. amazement
3. reenter
4. relation
5. careful
6. prepay
7. useful
8. taking
9. misplace
10. unnatural
11. inborn
12. cooperate
13. hopeless
14. spacious
15. pavement
16. mistrust
17. unknown
18. joking
19. storage
20. nameless

Page 471, Exercise

1. dirtier
2. happily
3. staying
4. sprayer
5. hurrying
6. glorious
7. prayer
8. laziest
9. shininess
10. enjoyment
11. skinnier
12. mysterious
13. thirtieth
14. dutiful
15. sleepier
16. merriment
17. joyous
18. silliest
19. carriage
20. employer

Page 472, Exercise A

1. carefully
2. unevenness
3. beautifully
4. fanned
5. neared
6. wrapped
7. running
8. Practically
9. openness
10. actually, sitting

Page 472, Exercise B

1. evenness
2. cruelly
3. plugging
4. planned
5. remittance
6. slimmer
7. tugging
8. loaned
9. treating
10. sleeping
11. bashfully
12. trimmed
13. swimmer
14. merrily
15. fatter
16. heating
17. leanness
18. sooner
19. slugger
20. dragging

Page 473, Exercise

1. ceded
2. shield
3. piece
4. preceded
5. relieve
6. seized
7. proceeded
8. exceed
9. ceiling
10. niece

1. desert
2. dessert
3. Capitol
4. here
5. its
6. It's
7. lose
8. loose
9. principal
10. stationary

Page 476, Exercise B

1. their
2. there
3. too
4. Two
5. weather
6. whether
7. Who's
8. whose
9. Your
10. You're

Page 477, Review

1. unusual
2. misunderstand, proposal
3. reaction, disappointment
4. hopelessly
5. useless, chopping
6. busiest
7. cities
8. beautiful, lovelier
9. feared, meanness
10. repeated, totally
11. sitting
12. received, biggest
13. succeeds, self-reliant
14. exceeded
15. believes, taking
16. hear
17. principal
18. their
19. too
20. your

HANDBOOK SECTION 16

The Correct Form for Writing

Page 482, Exercise

1. Kristen drove 600 miles and spent only nineteen dollars on gasoline.
2. One hundred twenty-six beds were added in the new wing of the hospital.
3. Check page 42 for the answer to the fourth question.
4. Our doctor's office is at 600 West Seventh Street in Room 82.
5. San Diego's average temperature for January is 56 degrees.
6. The first postage stamp sold on July 1, 1847, for five cents.
7. The bike Jake wanted cost eighty dollars.
8. Earth, the fifth largest planet, revolves around the sun at a rate of 17.5 miles per minute.
9. I called the weather service at WE6–1660 and found out that the temperature is 80 degrees.
10. Two percent of the people in the United States are farmers.

Page 483, Exercise

1. The FCC granted a license to a new radio station in Eugene, Oregon.
2. Ms. Albers introduced Calvin Olby, Jr., the president of Dixie Company.
3. Lt. Reilly saluted the captain.
4. In December, basketball season begins for the year.
5. On Tuesday, November 4, the polls will open at 6:00 A.M.
6. The address of the White House is 1600 Pennsylvania Avenue.
7. The cacti in Arizona often reach fifty feet in height.
8. The Department of Energy building in Maryland is hard to find.
9. Mr. Rhodes explained Monday's assignment of pages 66 to 69 in the social studies textbook.
10. Wounded Knee, South Dakota, was the site of a major conflict.

Application for Employment

Personal Information

Date _____   Social Security Number _____

Name _____
          Last   First   Middle

Present Address _____
          Street   City   State   Zip

Phone Number _____   Date of Birth _____   U.S. Citizen   Yes   No

Employment Desired

Position _____   Date You Can Start _____   Salary Desired _____

Are You Employed Now? _____ Where? _____ Duties _____

Education	Name and Location of School	Years Attended	Date Graduated	Course of Study
Grammar School				
High School				
College or Trade School				
Military Service				

Former Employers *(List your last two employers, starting with the more recent one)*

Dates		Name and Address of Employer	Salary	Position	Reason for Leaving
From	To				
From	To				

References *Name two persons, not related to you, who have known you at least one year.*

Name	Address	Business

In Case of Emergency
Notify _____
          Name   Address   Phone No.

I authorize investigation of all statements contained in this application. I understand that misrepresentation or omission of facts called for is cause for dismissal.

Date _____   Signature of Applicant _____